MR. JEFFERSON'S DECLARATION

MR. JEFFERSON'S DECLARATION

THE STORY
BEHIND THE DECLARATION
OF INDEPENDENCE

By Frank Donovan

ILLUSTRATED

DODD, MEAD & COMPANY
NEW YORK

77769

Permission to quote from the volumes below is gratefully acknowledged:

The Story of the Declaration of Independence by Dumas Malone.
Quoted by permission of the Oxford University Press, London, Copyright 1954.

The Declaration of Independence by Carl Becker. Published by Alfred A. Knopf, Inc. New York, N. Y. Copyright 1922 by Carl Becker. Renewed 1942.

Puritanism and Democracy by Ralph Barton Perry. Quoted by permission of the Vanguard Press. New York, N. Y. Copyright 1944.

Jefferson the Virginian by Dumas Malone. Quoted by permission of Little, Brown and Company, Boston, Mass. Copyright 1948.

973.313
Don

Donald March 1968 $4.19

Contents

Contents

Illustrations

MR. JEFFERSON'S DECLARATION

In some instances the archaic spelling and punctuation in quotations have been modernized for clarity, but they have been retained where they are essential to the text.

1

The Road to Independence

If public opinion polls had existed in colonial days, they would have disclosed history's most drastic swing in political opinion. The query, "Do you think that the colonies in America should be independent of Great Britain?", would have brought a resounding "No!" from a large majority of Americans, almost down to the day on which independence was declared. Certainly, up to four or five months before July 2, 1776, the bulk of the people would have expressed themselves in the negative.

Nobody wanted independence—or so they said. Opposition to the iniquities of British rule grew steadily for twelve years before the fighting started; roughly from the end of the French and Indian War in 1763. But the Whigs, who led this opposition, constantly and consistently reiterated the solemn affirmation that the only object of their agitation was the correction of the specific grievances resulting from a bad ministerial policy in Great Britain. The idea of independence was, they said, abhorrent and it was calumny to accuse them of such thoughts.

The Stamp Act Congress, in 1765, declared that the colonies' connection with Great Britain was "their greatest happiness and security," and that they "most ardently" desired its "perpetual continuance." Even the most radical of the Whigs endorsed this principle. One such was James Otis who, in January, 1768, drafted instructions to Massachusetts' agent, protesting Parliament's taxation policy, in which he said: "We cannot justly be suspected of the most distant thought of Independency of Great Britain. Some, we know, have imagined this . . . but it is so far from the truth that we apprehend the colonies would refuse it if offered to them, and would even deem it the greatest misfortune to be obliged to accept it." In 1774, when the Massachusetts House of Representatives sent delegates to the First Continental Congress, instructions signed by another radical leader, Samuel Adams, declared: "the restoration of union and harmony between Great Britain and the colonies [was] most ardently desired by all good men." And that same first Continental Congress, in its solemn petition to the King, adopted in October, 1774, professed the most devoted loyalty: "We wish not a diminution of the prerogative. . . . Your royal authority over us and our connection with Great Britain we shall always carefully and zealously endeavor to support and maintain." In March, 1775, Benjamin Franklin said, in London, that he had never heard in America one word in favor of independence, "from any person, drunk or sober."

Even after the fighting started in April, 1775, the colonials insisted that they were not contesting for independence. When George Washington was en route to the Continental Congress, a month later, he met a friend who warned him that what he was doing might lead to civil war and an effort for independence; to which Washington replied, said his friend, "that if I ever heard of his joining in any such measures, I had his leave to set him down for everything wicked." On July 6, 1775, less than a year before independence was proclaimed, Congress adopted a declaration "setting forth the causes and necessity of our taking up arms"—drafted in part by Thomas Jefferson—in which they proclaimed: "lest this declaration should disquiet the minds of our friends and fellow subjects in any part of the empire, we assure them that we mean not to dissolve that union which has so long and so happily subsisted us, and which we sincerely wish to see restored. . . . We have not raised armies, with ambitious designs of separating us from Great Britain, and established independent states."

More than two months after the Battle of Bunker Hill and less than nine months before he would write his famous Declaration, Thomas Jefferson wrote to a kinsman that he was "looking with fondness toward a reconciliation with Great Britain." In January, 1776, New Hampshire incorporated in its new constitution a disavowal of any purpose aiming at independence. In that same month, New York, New Jersey, Pennsylvania, and Maryland specifically instructed their delegates to the Continental Congress, to vote against any resolution having to do with severing relations with Great Britain.

The situation at the beginning of 1776 was aptly summarized by Thomas Paine, when he wrote, a few years later:

"I happened to come to America a few months before the breaking out of hostilities. I found the disposition of the people such that they might have been led by a thread and governed by a reed. Their suspicion was quick and penetrating, but their attachment to Britain was obstinate, and it was at that time a kind of treason to speak against it. They disliked the Ministry, but they esteemed the nation. Their idea of grievance operated without resentment, and their single object was reconciliation."

The Second Continental Congress, which proclaimed independence, usually numbered thirty-five to forty members in attendance. Delegates came and went, depending on conditions in their home colonies; they frequently went home to attend to local public business that they considered more important than national affairs. At times some colonies were not represented at all, and others by only one member. In January of 1776 there were only seven men in the Congress who to that time had spoken for independence: Wythe of Virginia, Gadsen of South Carolina, McKean of Delaware, Franklin of Pennsylvania, Ward of Rhode Island, Deane of Connecticut, and Samuel Adams of Massachusetts. True, these would soon be augmented by other radicals, including Sherman of Connecticut, John Adams of Massachusetts, and, in March, Richard Henry Lee of Virginia. Still, as late as March or April, the liberals could not have secured a majority for a resolution of independence. Yet, three months later, Congress was unanimous in voting for total separation from the mother country.

The causes of the American Revolution, which also led to the decision for independence, have been the subject of many weighty and erudite tomes that explain the complexities of the political, social, philosophical, and economic relationships of the colonies and the mother country. Actually, the grievances of which the colonies complained most vehemently had to do with but one thing—money. At the outset, at least, "liberty," "freedom," "the rights of man," and other such fine phrases were words employed to protest some action of the mother country that was aimed at depriving her children of money.

Edmund Burke, champion of the colonial cause in Parliament, made this point but a few weeks before the American Revolution reached the shooting stage. He said that, in England, "the great contests for freedom . . . were from the earliest times chiefly upon the question of taxing. Most of the contests in the ancient commonwealths turned primarily on the right of election of magistrates, or on the balance among the several orders of the state. The question of money was not, with them, so immediate. But in England it was otherwise. On this point of taxes the ablest pens and most eloquent tongues have been exercised, the greatest spirits have acted and suffered. . . . They took infinite pains to inculcate, as a fundamental principle, that in all monarchies the people themselves must, in effect, mediately or immediately, possess the power of granting their own money, or no shadow of liberty could subsist. The colonies draw from you, as with their lifeblood, these ideas and principles. Their love of liberty, as with you, fixed and attached on this specific point of taxing. Liberty might be safe or might be endangered in twenty other particulars without their being much pleased or alarmed. Here they felt its pulse; and as they found that beat, they thought themselves sick or sound."

Prior to the ascension to the throne of George III, in 1760, the colonies had largely been allowed to grow up neglected. True, there were some thirty laws designed, in accordance with the mercantile policy of the day, to control the commerce and productions of the colonies for the benefit of England, but these were seldom stringently enforced and the colonies ignored or circumvented them without complaint. The first specific protest which received much public attention was that of James Otis, in 1761. The Massachusetts lawyer argued against the use of "writs of assistance" as a means of repressing smuggling in his colony. Otis claimed that this act of Parliament was contrary to natural law and therefore unconstitutional and void. In fact, the colonies would have protested *any* vigorous effort to repress smuggling which, they seemed to feel, was an "inalienable right" of free men.

The analogy has been made that the colonies on mainland America were allowed to grow through their infancy and their teens without much supervision from home. The insular colonies in the West Indies, commercially more important in the early years, had been brought up under proper homeland discipline, but those along the coast had been allowed to fend for themselves. Now, as they reached maturity, Mother England suddenly realized that they were potential wage earners and wanted them to contribute to the support of the home. The American colonists, who had come through the difficult teen years on their own, had developed a self-reliance and an independence that resisted discipline. They had never received adequate board and lodging and they now had no intention of paying rent.

Until 1763, such laws as Parliament had passed dealt

mainly with the regulation of commerce. The imperial theory was that the colonies should be sources of raw materials for the mother country, at favorable prices, and customers for English manufactured goods, at inflated prices. All trade must be with the mother country, in English bottoms. Tobacco, for instance, for which there was a good market in Holland, had to be consigned to an English merchant, shipped to England, unloaded and reshipped by him to the Dutch. There was a thriving market for beaver hats in Europe, but the colonists were allowed to make hats only for themselves; beaver skins had to be shipped raw and processed in England. The same was true with iron, the ore for which abounded in the colonies. It could be processed in the New World to the point of pigs, but further forming must be done in the mother country, which would ship the finished product back to the colonies at a handsome profit.

When the French and Indian War ended in 1763, England was faced with an enormous postwar debt. There was a strong feeling in the heavily taxed mother country that the colonies, which benefited most by the exclusion of the French from North America, should pay part of it, and that they should meet some of the expense of maintaining British armed forces in America to protect the frontier. In 1764, Parliament passed the American Revenue Act—generally known as the Sugar Act—for the specific purpose of raising money in the colonies for the Crown. There was nothing new about this; it had to do with import duties. The trouble was that the British were determined to enforce it by revitalizing the customs service. To that time the American customs had returned little more than one fourth of the cost of collecting them.

Another unpopular British measure was an act that prohibited the colonists from settling west of the Appalachians. This land, said Parliament, was to be Indian domain, to be acquired, if at all, by negotiations between the British and the redskins. Here, too, money was at the root of the colonists' complaint—free land and the profitable fur trade.

For the purpose of producing revenue for England, the Sugar Act was followed, in 1765, by the Stamp Act, the first direct tax ever levied by Parliament upon America. This was resisted violently on the grounds that Parliament had no right to levy internal taxes on the colonies. The phrase "taxation without representation" was on every tongue. The Stamp Act, it was said, violated the charters of the colonies; it violated the rights of free Englishmen who, under the British constitution, could be taxed only by their own consent. Internal affairs in the colonies had always been handled by the colonial legislatures, and only these could impose internal taxation.

There was much talk about the difference between internal and external taxation. The colonists claimed that they did not object to navigation and commercial regulatory acts, even though they incidently raised revenue for the mother country. It might be added that the extent of their lack of objection paralleled the extent of the lack of enforcement. But they insisted that Parliament had no right to levy internal taxes. Benjamin Franklin, when examined at the bar of the House of Commons, in 1766, stressed this distinction between internal and external taxation, but admitted that no such distinction was expressed in the words of the colonial charters. When asked whether the colonists might not object also to Parliament's right to external taxation, he replied; "They never have, hitherto. Many arguments have been lately used here to shew them that there is no difference, and that if you have no right to tax them internally, you have no right to tax them externally, or make any other law to bind them. At present they do not reason so, but in time they may possibly be convinced by these arguments."

Another act that caused dissatisfaction in the colonies—also involving money—was the Quartering Act of 1765. This provided that the civil authorities in the colonies had to contribute to the support of British troops in America. This led to one of the early open acts of rebellion when, in 1766, the New York assembly refused to vote an appropriation for maintaining the British forces in that colony and was, in consequence, temporarily prorogued.

The ineffectual Stamp Act was repealed in 1766. In the rejoicing at this victory for the colonies little attention was paid to the Declaratory Act that went with the repeal and which proclaimed that Parliament: "had, hath, and of right ought to have, full power and authority to make laws and statutes of sufficient force and validity to bind the colonies and people of America, subjects of the crown of Great Britain, in all cases whatsoever." Despite the popular protest against taxation without representation that was hurled at every revenue-producing act of the Parliament, there was small furore about this parliamentary act, which specifically claimed such a right—but did not impose any taxes.

As a revenue producer the Stamp Act was superseded by the Townshend Acts, in 1767. The new Chancellor of the Exchequer, Charles Townshend, thought to hoodwink the colonies by apparently conforming to their position on external taxation. He hoped to raise some £40,000 by import duties on glass, lead, paints, paper, and tea. Further, he provided for efficient collection of the new duties by strengthening the customs service. It was to this last provision that the colonists took greatest exception. They resisted the Townshend Acts with a renewal of the policy of nonimportation of British goods; a policy that had proved effective against both the Sugar Act and its enforcement program and the Stamp Act. The Townshend Acts had the effect of demonstrating that *any* parliamentary taxation whatever would be unacceptable to the Americans. It was no longer a case of "taxation without representation"; it was, simply, "no taxation."

Thus the situation stood in 1768. In addition to economic sanctions through nonimportation, there had been some active instances of resistance, starting in 1765 with the formation of secret organizations in several colonies, known as Sons of Liberty. Although some of these were organized by mature men of good reputation, the nature of their actions was such that one is tempted to believe that their rank and file may have been largely hell-raising youth. They erected liberty poles, harassed customs officials, forced agents under the Stamp Act to resign or flee, with the threat or use of tar and feathers. They burned admiralty court records, ransacked the home of the comptroller of currency in Boston, and looted the home and library of Massachusetts Chief Justice Hutchinson. In the New York Quartering Act crisis, they fought a pitched battle with redcoats who cut down their liberty pole. When John Hancock's sloop, the *Liberty*, was seized by the customs for smuggling Madeira wine, they assaulted the customs officials on the dock and drove them to seek refuge in Castle William, from whence they appealed for troops.

On the nonviolent side, in addition to economic sanctions, colonial resistance was evidenced by the Stamp Act Congress, attended by nine colonies, and by a rash of Whig pamphlets setting forth the rights of the colonies. Most famous of these were John Dickinson's "Letters from a Farmer in Pennsylvania to the Inhabitants of the British Colonies," which, in 1776, conceded Parliament's right to regulate trade, even if revenue was incidentally produced thereby, but denied its right to pass laws specifically for raising revenue and assailed the suspension of the New York assembly as a blow to the liberty of all the colonies. Although they were widely read in America and abroad, when published in pamphlet form, the more radical Whig thinking was already in advance of Dickinson by this time.

More effective, perhaps, in the progress toward union was the Massachusetts Circular Letter, drafted by Samuel Adams in 1768, which denounced the Townshend Acts and solicited proposals for united action. Although the British Secretary of State for the Colonies ordered royal governors to dissolve colonial assemblies, if necessary, to prevent them from endorsing the letter, it was approved by the legislative bodies of New Hampshire, Connecticut, and New Jersey; Virginia drew its own Circular Letter advising support of Massachusetts.

In 1768 two regiments of British troops were landed in Boston to support the customs authorities. The widespread resentment against these lobster-backs had, in part, an economic basis. The miserably paid redcoats sought to moonlight in off-duty hours, which roused the opposition of

Boston labor. The riot in 1770, which American history has labeled the Boston Massacre, started with a dispute on this score—a fistfight between a worker in a rope yard and a British soldier who was seeking employment. The fistfight developed into a small riot and then, that night, into a larger one in which a crowd attacked a British sentry. A guard of six men came to support him, fired a volley, and killed five Bostonians.

In 1770 the Townshend Acts were repealed, except for the duty on tea, which was retained as a token of England's right to impose import duties. From this point on, political differences, as opposed to purely economic ones, became an increasingly important factor in the resentment of the colonies. When, in 1772, Rhode Island colonists captured and burned the British revenue cutter, *Gaspé*, the case was ordered to be tried in an admiralty court in England, without a jury. The colonists saw this as a violation of a long-standing, basic right, under their own and the British constitution. Then, Governor Hutchinson of Massachusetts announced that henceforth his salary and that of Massachusetts judges would be paid by the Crown rather than the colony, thus making the executive and the judiciary independent of the colonial legislature. Events such as these led to the formation, in Massachusetts, of a twenty-one-man Committee of Correspondence to make her position clear to other colonies and "to the World." By February, 1774, all of the other colonies, except North Carolina and Pennsylvania, had set up similar committees to propagandize the radical Whig point of view.

In December, 1773, occurred the incident of violence that turned out to be determinative. The previous year Parliament had passed the Tea Act to save the East India Company from bankruptcy. The company, whose influence in India was very important to the Crown, had seventeen million pounds of tea in English warehouses and the bottom dropped out of the market. The Tea Act permitted them to sell this tea in the colonies, through special consignees, without payment of export duties. (This did not effect the import duty in the colonies.) Under these conditions the consignees could undersell colonial merchants who had imported tea honestly, as well as the more numerous ones who were handling tea smuggled from Holland. It was this threat of a British-controlled trade monopoly, rather than the import duty on tea (which was then six years old) that aroused the ire of the colonies. In Philadelphia a town meeting induced the tea consignees to resign their commissions. In New York the Sons of Liberty terrorized the consignees to the same end. In Charlestown the tea was landed, confiscated for nonpayment of import duty and later sold by the revolutionary government to support the war effort. But in Boston a shipload of tea was dramatically dumped into the harbor by a group of men ridiculously disguised as Mohawk Indians.

From this point on, the actions of the British Crown seemed to be calculated to force the colonies into rebellion. In the spring of 1774, Parliament met in an angry mood. George III had expressed a personal wish that Massachusetts be punished for the Tea Party in particular and her long list of rebellious acts in general. Parliament passed the Intolerable Acts, aimed at punishing Massachusetts. The port of Boston was declared closed to commerce. Another act reorganized the government of Massachusetts so as to increase

the powers of the Crown, at the expense of the colonial
legislature. A third broadened the Quartering Act. Another
provided that trials for murder committed by Crown officials in the course of subduing riots should be held in England or another colony. At the same time the Quebec Act
was passed, extending the boundaries of that province to the
Ohio River and taking from the other colonies western lands
which they claimed under their original charters.

The colonies were aroused as they had not been since the
passage of the Stamp Act nine years earlier. Rhode Island,
followed by New York and Pennsylvania, called for an
intercolony congress to consider the rights and grievances
of all the colonies. On September 5, 1774, fifty-six delegates
from twelve colonies—Georgia was not represented—met in
Carpenters Hall in Philadelphia as the First Continental
Congress.

The most important act of this Congress was the adoption of ten resolutions embodying a declaration of the
political rights claimed by the colonies. The demand was
based upon a threefold foundation: the "natural rights" of
mankind, the constitutional rights of Englishmen, the specific rights granted in colonial charters. The resolution
stated: "That they were entitled to life, liberty, and property, and that they have never ceded to any sovereign power
whatever, a right to dispose of either without their consent."
The resolutions denounced the Coercive Acts as unjust,
cruel, and unconstitutional. They criticized the interference
with trial by jury through the extension of admiralty court
jurisdiction; the dissolution of colonial assemblies; the maintenance of a standing army in the colonies in peacetime;
and the exercise of legislative power by a council appointed

by the Crown. They maintained that colonial legislatures were entitled to exclusive power of legislation, subject to the traditional veto of the Crown. The greatest subject of dispute, within the Congress, was what authority, if any, Parliament should have in matters of taxation. A compromise resolution on this point, written by John Adams, stated that the colonial legislatures should have jurisdiction in "all cases of taxation and internal policy," and added, "from the necessity of the case, and a regard to the mutual interest of both countries, we cheerfully consent to the operation of such acts of the British Parliament as are *bona fide* restrained to the regulation of our external commerce . . . excluding every idea of taxation, internal or external, for raising a revenue on the subjects in America without their consent."

The first Congress adopted only three "peaceable measures" to obtain redress of colonial grievances; the old reliable nonimportation, which was imposed on all the colonies and extended to include nonexportation to Great Britain, an address to the people of Great Britain, and a loyal address to the King.

A sidelight of this Congress was the expression of several political viewpoints proposing what amounted to dominion status for the colonies, along the same lines as the later development of Canada in its relation to the British Commonwealth. James Wilson of Pennsylvania expressed this in his "Considerations of the Nature and Extent of the Legislative Authority of the British Parliament." Thomas Jefferson had already expressed it in his *Summary View of the Rights of British America*. John Adams virtually proposed dominion status in his *Novanglus* letters, written shortly after the Congress adjourned. Parliament, said Adams, had no authority over the colonies; "Massachusetts is a realm, New York is a realm," over which the King is sovereign.

By the time the Second Continental Congress met for its first session on May 10, 1775, the "shot heard 'round the world" had been fired at Concord. The makeup of this body was somewhat more radical than that of the First Congress. Delegates were appointed or elected by colonial legislatures or conventions, which reflected public opinion. The fact that conservatives like Galloway of Pennsylvania and Low of New York were absent, replaced by liberals like Franklin and Wilson of Pennsylvania, Hancock of Massachusetts and, later, Jefferson of Virginia, was an indication that the Whig forces were gathering grass-roots strength. Still, a large majority of the Congress was conservative. Although active fighting was in progress, in which England was clearly the aggressor, there was no mention of independence in the proceedings of this session. Instead, Congress approved John Dickinson's Olive Branch Petition, which professed the attachment of the American people to George III, expressed their hope for the restoration of harmony, and implored the King to prevent further hostile actions against the colonies until a reconciliation could be worked out. The "Declaration of the Causes and Necessities of Taking up Arms" also rejected independence, but asserted that Americans were ready to die rather than be enslaved.

When Congress reconvened for its second session in September, 1775, no answer had been received to the Olive Branch Petition. In fact, on the very day he was to have received it, the King had issued a proclamation declaring that "open and avowed rebellion existed in the colonies." In a later warlike speech to Parliament, George III denounced the colonists who, he said, "openly avow their revolt, hostility, and rebellion." The King was among the first to raise the spectre of independence when he said; "The rebellious war now levied is become more general, and is manifestly carried on for the purpose of establishing an independent Empire." Parliament added fuel to the flames by the passage of an act declaring the colonies out of the King's protection, prohibiting all trade with America, and authorizing forfeiture of captured ships and property as enemy property. In short, the Parliament more or less proclaimed the colonies as an independent enemy rather than rebellious subjects.

During the early days of 1776, news of these events reached Congress, together with word that the British had burned Norfolk and that 12,000 German mercenaries were en route to the New World, to subdue the colonies. This was considered a particularly barbaric act, since it was wrongly assumed that these mercenaries would not be governed by the rules of civilized warfare. The public mind was inflamed with visions of rape, looting, pillage, arson, and vandalism.

All of these occurrences, early in the new year, might be compared to a chemical process in which several diverse elements needed only a catalyst to fuse them into a single compound. The catalyst was provided in January, 1776, by the publication of Thomas Paine's *Common Sense*. This 25,000-word pamphlet was an immediate, runaway best seller. It contained a passionate appeal for independence, couched in language that the man in the street could readily understand. It presented no subtle, philosophical, political theorizing. Rather, it condemned monarchy, argued the futility of reconciliation, and presented the practical benefits of independence in terms of simple reason—of, as the name implied, common sense.

Paine started with a discussion on the "origin and design of government in general," which, he said, was at best a necessary evil and "in its worst state, an intolerable one." He gave an example of primitive government in its simplest forms, ending with: "Here, then, is the origin and rise of government; namely, a mode rendered necessary by the inability of moral virtue to govern the world; here, too, is the design and end of government, viz., freedom and security."

Of all types of government, said Paine, monarchy was the worst. Government by kings was: "the most prosperous invention the devil ever set on foot for the promotion of idolatry. The heathen paid divine honors to their deceased kings, and the Christian world has improved on the plan by doing the same to their living ones. How impious is the title of sacred majesty applied to a worm, who in the midst of his splendor is crumbling into dust." And of all kings, England's had less claim to the right to rule than most. "England since the conquest hath known some few good monarchs, but groaned beneath a much larger number of bad ones; yet no man in his senses can say that their claim under William the Conqueror is a very honorable one. A French bastard landing with an armed *banditti* and establishing himself King of England against the consent of the natives, is in plain terms a very paltry rascally original. It certainly hath no divinity in it. . . . In England a king hath little more to do than to make war and give away places; which, in plain terms, is to empoverish the nation and set it together by the ears. A pretty business indeed for a man to be allowed eight hundred thousand sterling a year for, and worshipped into the bargain! Of more worth is one honest man to society, and in the sight of God, than all the crowned ruffians that ever lived."

This diatribe against monarchy was followed by "Thoughts on the Present State of Affairs in America," in which Paine first proved that reconciliation with Great Britain was absurd, impossible, and if it were possible, thoroughly undesirable. He then showed that independence was the only common-sense course open to the colonists—and now was the time, for: "The sun never shone on a cause of greater worth. 'Tis not the affair of a city, a county, a province, or a kingdom, but of a continent—of at least one-eighth part of the habitable globe. 'Tis not the concern of a day, a year, or an age; posterity are virtually involved in the contest, and will be more or less affected even to the end of time, by the proceedings now. Now is the seedtime of continental union, faith, and honor. The least fracture now will be like a name engraved with the point of a pin on the tender rind of a young oak; the wound would enlarge with the tree, and posterity read it in full-grown characters."

Thoughts of reconciliation might have been proper in the past, but: "All plans, proposals, &c, prior to the nineteenth of April; i.e., to the commencement of hostilities, are like the almanacs of the last year, which, though proper then, are superseded and useless now." In any event, reconciliation which would restore dependence on Great Britain was a shortsighted policy that was not in the best interests of the colonies, and Paine proceeded to knock down the arguments advanced for it.

There were those that said that America had flourished

under her connection with Great Britain in the past, and
that such a connection was necessary for future prosperity.
Nothing could be more fallacious, said Paine, "We may as
well assert that because a child has thrived upon milk, that
it is never to have meat, or that the first twenty years of
our lives is to become a precedent for the next twenty. But
even this is admitting more than is true; for I answer
roundly, that America would have flourished as much, and
probably much more, had no European power taken any
notice of her. The commerce by which she hath enriched
herself are the necessaries of life, and will always have a
market while eating is the custom in Europe."

Great Britain had always protected the colonies, said
others. This Paine admitted, but added: "she would have
defended Turkey from the same motive; viz., for the sake
of trade and dominion . . . her motive was *interest* not
attachment; and . . . she did not protect us from *our enemies* on *our account,* but from *her enemies* on *her own
account.* . . . France and Spain never were, nor perhaps ever
will be, our enemies as *Americans,* but as our being the *subjects of Great Britain.*"

Some say that Britain is the parent country. "Then the
more shame on her conduct. Even brutes do not devour
their young, nor savages make war upon their families;
wherefore, the assertion, if true, turns to her reproach; but
it happens not to be true, or only partly so, and the phrase
parent or *mother country* hath been jesuistically adopted by
the King and his parasites, with a low papistical design of
gaining an unfair bias on the credulous weakness of our
minds. Europe, and not England, is the parent country of
America. This New World hath been the asylum for the

persecuted lovers of civil and religious liberty from *every part of Europe*. Hither have they fled, not from the tender embraces of the mother, but from the cruelty of the monster; and it is so far true of England, that the same tyranny which drove the first emigrants from home, pursues their descendants still."

Most of Paine's arguments were economic rather than philosophical. Separation from England was simply good business. "Our plan is commerce, and that, well attended to, will secure us the peace and friendship of all Europe, because it is the interest of all Europe to have America a free port. Her trade will always be a protection, and her barrenness of gold and silver secure her from invaders.

"I challenge the warmest advocate for reconciliation to show a single advantage that this continent can reap by being connected with Great Britain. I repeat the challenge: not a single advantage is derived. Our corn will fetch its price in any market in Europe, and our imported goods must be paid for, buy them where we will."

In addition, England could not govern the American colonists from so far away, and with her ignorance of the interests of the colonies: "To be always running three or four thousand miles with a tale or a petition, waiting four or five months for an answer, which, when obtained, requires five or six more to explain it in, will in a few years be looked upon as folly and childishness. There was a time when it was proper, and there is a proper time for it to cease." Further, it was ridiculous for a small island to try to rule a large continent. "America is only a secondary object in the system of British politics. England consults the good of this country no further than it answers her own purpose. Wherefore, her own interest leads her to suppress the growth of ours in every case which doth not promote her advantage, or in the least interferes with it."

The only reasonable course, said Paine, was separation from Great Britain. " 'Tis repugnant to reason, to the universal order of things, to all examples from former ages, to suppose that this continent can long remain subject to any external power. The most sanguine in Britain doth not think so. The utmost stretch of human wisdom cannot, at this time, compass a plan, short of separation, which can promise the continent even a year's security. Reconciliation is *now* a fallacious dream. Nature has deserted the connection, and art cannot supply her place. For, as Milton wisely expresses, 'never can true reconcilement grow where wounds of deadly hate have pierced so deep. . . .' Wherefore, since nothing but blows will do, for God's sake let us come to a final separation, and not leave the next generation to be cutting throats under the violated unmeaning names of parent and child."

Common Sense then presented arguments to show that the colonies could stand on their own feet. " 'Tis not in numbers but in unity that our great strength lies; yet our present numbers are sufficient to repel the force of all the world. The continent has at this time the largest body of armed and disciplined men of any power under heaven; and is just arrived at that pitch of strength, in which no single colony is able to support itself, and the whole, when united, is able to do anything." True, the country had no navy, but Paine showed that it could easily build one. It also had no debts. It had a wealth of unoccupied land. "No nation on earth hath such an advantage as this." And it had youth. "Youth is the seedtime of good habits as well in nations as in individuals. It might be difficult, if not impossible, to form the continent into one government half a century hence."

"To conclude," said Paine, "however strange it may appear to some, or however unwilling they may be to think so, matters not, but many strong and striking reasons may be given to show that nothing can settle our affairs so expeditiously as an open and determined DECLARATION FOR INDEPENDENCE." He then gave four reasons why a declaration of independence was desirable. The first three had to do with foreign aid, which the colonies could not expect while they were in the position of rebels. In the fourth reason, Paine virtually described the Declaration of Independence that would come forth six months after his pamphlet was published. "Were a manifesto to be published, and despatched to foreign courts, setting forth the miseries we have endured, and the peaceful methods which we have ineffectually used for redress, declaring at the same time, that not being able any longer to live happily or safely under the cruel disposition of the British court, we had been driven to the necessity of breaking off all connections with her; at the same time, assuring all such courts of our peaceable disposition towards them, and of our desire of entering into trade with them. Such a memorial would produce more good effects to this continent, than if a ship were freighted with petitions to Britain."

Common Sense burst like a bombshell on the American scene. The authorized editions sold some 120,000 copies in three months. In the absence of copyright laws, there were numerous pirate editions; the total sale has been variously estimated at 300,000 to 500,000 in an area where there were probably not more than 600,000 families. It was reviewed by every newspaper and led to a rash of articles on independence. It was read by schoolteachers to their classes, by speakers to illiterate audiences, by officers in the army to the troops.

Throughout the colonies, letters and editorials attested to the marvelous influence of Paine's pamphlet. From Maryland: "If anyone knows the author of *Common Sense*, tell him he has done wonders and worked miracles—made Tories Whigs and washed blackamoors white." From South Carolina: "The author of *Common Sense* . . . deserves a statue of gold." From New York: "The ineffable delight with which it is perused and its doctrine imbibed is a demonstration that the seeds of independence, though imported with the troops from Britain, will grow surprisingly with proper cultivation in the fields of America." From Massachusetts, by the pen of Abigail Adams: "I am charmed with the sentiments of *Common Sense* and wonder how an honest heart . . . can hesitate one moment in adopting them." From North Carolina: "*Common Sense* hath made Independents of the majority of the country." From Cambridge, George Washington wrote: "My countrymen, I know, from their form of government and steady attachment heretofore to royalty, will come reluctantly into the idea of Independence, but time and persecution bring many wonderful things to pass; and by private letters which I have lately received from Virginia, I find *Common Sense* is working a powerful change there in the minds of men."

On the very day that Congress first considered the subject of independence, June 7, William Gordon, historian of the

Revolution, thus described the influence of *Common Sense* in preparing the minds of the people for this event: "Nothing could have been better timed than this performance. In unison with the sentiments and feelings of the people, it has produced most astonishing effects, and been received with vast applause, read by almost every American, and recommended as a work replete with truth, and against which none but the partial and prejudiced can form any objections. It has satisfied multitudes that it is their true interest immediately to cut the Gordian knot by which the American colonies have been bound to Great Britain, and to open their commerce, as an independent people, to all the nations of the world. It has been greatly instrumental in producing a similarity of sentiment through the continent, upon the subject under the consideration of Congress."

During the late winter and spring of 1776, there was a complete revolution of popular opinion in relation to independence, which was reflected in the mood of state legislatures. In April the North Carolina Provisional Congress instructed that colony's delegates to join with other colonies in voting for independence at the forthcoming meeting of the Continental Congress. Rhode Island gave its members carte blanche. In May a Virginia convention adopted a resolution instructing that colony's delegates in Congress to "propose to that respectable body to declare the United Colonies free and independent states."

Before these instructions reached the Virginia delegates in Congress, that body, on May 15, declared independence through the back door, so to speak. Several colonies had asked for opinions or instructions on the setting up of local governments. The Congress now passed a resolution, with a preamble written by John Adams, which read:

"Whereas His Britannic Majesty, in conjunction with the lords and commons of Great Britain, has, by a late act of Parliament, excluded the inhabitants of these United Colonies from the protection of his crown. And, whereas, no answer whatever, to the humble petitions of the colonies for redress of grievances and reconciliation with Great Britain has been or is likely to be given; but, the whole force of that kingdom, aided by foreign mercenaries, is to be exerted for the destruction of the good people of these colonies. And whereas, it appears absolutely irreconcilable to reason and good conscience, for the people of these colonies now to take the oaths and affirmations necessary for the support of any government under the crown of Great Britain, and it is necessary that the exercise of every kind of authority under the said crown should be totally suppressed, and all the powers of government exerted, under the authority of the people of the colonies, for the preservation of internal peace, virtue, and good order, as well as for the defense of their lives, liberties, and properties, against the hostile invasions and cruel depredations of their enemies; therefore:

"Resolved, that it be recommended to the respective assemblies and conventions of the United Colonies, where no government sufficient to the exigencies of their affairs have been hitherto established, to adopt such government as shall, in the opinion of the representatives of the people, best conduce to the happiness and safety of their constituents in particular, and America in general."

John Adams, never one to hide his light under a bushel, later said that his preamble was "considered by men of understanding as equivalent to a declaration of independence." At the time he wrote to his wife, Abigail: "Great Britain has at last driven America to the last step, a complete separation from her; a total absolute independence, not only of her Parliament, but of her Crown, for such is the amount of the resolve of the fifteenth."

On June 7, 1776, Richard Henry Lee of Virginia rose in the Congress to present the resolutions, three in number, which the convention in that colony had adopted the previous month, which read:

"THAT THESE UNITED COLONIES are, and of right ought to be free and independent states, that they are absolved from all allegiance to the British crown, and that all political connection between them and the state of Great Britain is, and ought to be totally dissolved.

"That it is expedient forthwith to take the most effectual measures for forming foreign alliances.

"That a plan of confederation be prepared and transmitted to the respective colonies for their consideration and approbation."

John Adams seconded the Virginia resolutions. Then the Congress declared itself a committee of the whole for debate, on which no minutes were kept. Perhaps the best account of what transpired between June 7 and June 10 is contained in Thomas Jefferson's autobiography:

"The House being obliged to attend at that time to some other business, the proposition was referred to the next day when the members were ordered to attend punctually at ten o'clock.

"Saturday, June 8. They proceeded to take it into consideration and referred it to a committee of the whole, into which they immediately resolved themselves, and passed that day and Monday, the tenth, in debating on the subject.

"It was argued by Wilson, Robert R. Livingston, E. Rutledge, Dickinson, and others:

"That though they were friends to the measures themselves, and saw the impossibility that we should ever again be united with Great Britain, yet they were against adopting them at this time.

"That the conduct we had formerly observed was wise and proper now, of deferring to take any capital step till the voice of the people drove us into it; that they were our power, and without them our declarations could not be carried into effect.

"That the people of the middle colonies (Maryland, Delaware, Pennsylvania, the Jerseys, and New York) were not yet ripe for bidding adieu to British connection, but that they were fast ripening, and in a short time would join in the general voice of America. . . .

"That if such a declaration should now be agreed to, these delegates must retire, and possibly their colonies might secede from the Union.

"That such a secession would weaken us more than could be compensated for by any foreign alliance.

"That in the event of such a division, foreign powers would either refuse to join themselves to our fortune, or having us so much in their power as that desperate declaration would place us, they would insist on terms proportionally more hard and prejudicial.

"That we had little reason to expect an alliance with those to whom alone as yet we had cast our eyes.

"That France and Spain had reason to be jealous of that

rising power which would one day certainly strip them of all their American possessions. . . .

"That it was prudent to fix among ourselves the terms on which we would form alliance, before we declared we would form one at all events.

"And that if these were agreed on, and our declaration of independence ready by the time our Ambassador should be prepared to sail, it would be as well to go into that declaration at this day.

"On the other side it was urged by J. Adams, (R.H.) Lee, Wythe, and others:

"That no gentleman had argued against the policy or the right of separation from Britain, nor had supposed it possible we should ever renew our connection, that they had only opposed its being now declared.

"That the question was not whether, by a declaration of independence, we should make ourselves what we are not; but whether we should declare a fact which already exists.

"That as to the people or Parliament of England, we had always been independent of them, their restraints on our trade deriving efficacy from our acquiescence only, and not from any rights they possessed of imposing them, and that so far our connection had been federal only and was now dissolved by the commencement of hostilities. . . .

"That the people wait for us to lead the way. . . .

"That it would be vain to wait either weeks or months for perfect unanimity, since it was impossible that all men should ever become of one sentiment on any question.

"That the conduct of some colonies from the beginning of this contest had given reason to suspect it was their settled policy to keep in the rear of the confederacy, that their particular prospect might be better even in the worst event.

"That, therefore, it was necessary for those colonies that had thrown themselves forward and hazarded all from the beginning, to come forward now also, and put all again to their own hazard. . . .

"That a declaration of independence alone could render it consistent with European delicacy for European powers to treat with us, or even to receive an Ambassador from us. . . .

"That though France and Spain may be jealous of our rising power, they must think it will be much more formidable with the addition of Great Britain, and will, therefore, see it [in] their interest to prevent a coalition; but should they refuse, we shall be but where we are, whereas without trying we shall never know whether they will aid us or not.

"That the present campaign may be unsuccessful, and, therefore, we had better propose an alliance while our affairs wear a hopeful aspect. . . .

"That it would be idle to lose time in settling the terms of alliance, till we had first determined we would enter into alliance. . . .

"It appearing in the course of these debates that the colonies of New York, Pennsylvania, Delaware, Maryland, and South Carolina were not yet matured for falling from the parent stem, but that they were fast advancing to that state, it was thought most prudent to wait a while for them, and to postpone the final decision to July 1."

On July 1, when the matter of independence was put to a vote, the first tally showed nine colonies in the affirmative. South Carolina and Pennsylvania were against. Only two of

Delaware's three delegates were present and these split. The instructions of New York's delegates prohibited them from voting on this issue without specific permission from home; they abstained. The final vote was put off until the next day, July 2. On that day two of Pennsylvania's four delegates who had voted in the negative, John Dickinson and William Morris, deliberately absented themselves, so that the three radical Pennsylvania members—Benjamin Franklin, James Wilson, and John Morton—were in the majority. South Carolina voted in the affirmative in the interest of unanimity. The third of Delaware's delegates, Caesar Rodney, gained a special niche in American history by riding eighty miles, night and day, through rain and thunder, to break the tie in his colony's small delegation and swing it into the affirmative column. New York still could not vote, but its delegates assured the Congress that their constituents would authorize them to vote favorably. The resolution was passed unanimously, pending the confirmation of New York, which was received by the Congress on July 15.

Writing the Declaration

Today, and for many generations past, almost every Independence Day speaker who mentions the Declaration of Independence uses the words "sacred" and "immortal." It is a sacred document, immortal because it proclaims the principles of liberty, the rights of man, and the philosophy of free government. But in the minds of the members of the Congress from which the Declaration issued there was no sacred purpose—no intention of creating an immortal document. The fame of the document that proclaimed independence—its sacredness and immortality—lay entirely in the future. The Congress planned merely a formal announcement of the resolution of independence, principally for purposes that were basically military. They wanted, as Jefferson wrote, to "let facts be submitted to a candid world," so that some part of that candid world would come to their assistance in fighting the British.

This is apparent in the debates on the resolution as described by Jefferson. Most of the arguments on both sides had to do with the probable effect of a declaration of independence on France and Spain. Opponents maintained that such a declaration would not help to gain the support of European powers "who had reason to be jealous of that rising power which would one day certainly strip them of all their American possessions"; that action should be deferred on a declaration until "our ambassador should be prepared to sail"; and that if some colonies did not endorse the Declaration, "foreign powers would either refuse to join themselves to our fortune, or having us so much in their power as that desperate Declaration would place us, would insist on terms proportionally more hard and prejudicial."

Proponents contended that "a declaration of independence alone would render it consistent with European delicacy for European powers to treat with us or even receive an ambassador from us," and that France and Spain would "see it in their interest" to prevent a coalition of the colonies and Great Britain. The Declaration should be made now, said its supporters, because the present military campaign "may be unsuccessful, and therefore we had better propose an alliance while our affairs wear a hopeful aspect."

It was obvious to all that the colonial military cause could not be successful without European support, at least in terms of money and arms. France and Spain were traditional enemies of England and would do anything they could to weaken the power of the island kingdom. They would also like a slice of the profitable trade with England's American colonies. But no European power would openly support the colonies so long as they were merely rebellious subjects of Great Britain. There was the possibility that such a difference might be settled by a reconciliation and a continuance of the colonies' allegiance to Great Britain. In this event England would undoubtedly turn against any power that had supported the colonies, with the former rebels on England's side—a situation that would put French or Spanish colonies in the New World in imminent danger.

Also, there was a psychological factor involved. Louis of France and Charles of Spain had no love for George of England—but they were fellow monarchs and, as such, could not in good conscience condone rebellious subjects, whose success might inspire others to like action, as it did. The revolutionary actions in which the French King lost his head and Spain lost her colonies in Latin America were sparked by the success of the revolution of the English colonists.

It would go against the grain for the Continental kings to support a rebellion against the insular king. Therefore, when seeking aid, it was desirable for the colonies to present themselves not as rebellious subjects but as an independent nation warring with another nation—to "assume among the powers of the earth a separate and equal station." In such a station they could properly seek allies whose interest would be served by their success. The writer of the Declaration had the difficult dual job of presenting convincing reasons to justify the rebellion of the colonies and at the same time creating the impression that it was not a rebellion—or, at least, that it was not a rebellion against rightful authority.

A secondary purpose of the Declaration, also military in

nature, was to inspire those at home to support the war effort—to delineate the cause for which they should come forward and fight. In this sense it was designed to be a rabble-rousing recruiting measure. The need for such a statement had been in the minds of Congress for some time. In May, 1776, they had appointed a committee consisting of Jefferson and George Wythe of Virginia, Samuel Adams of Massachusetts, and Edward Rutledge of South Carolina, to prepare an "animated address," which was to "impress the minds of the people with the necessity of now stepping forward to save their country, their freedom, and property." If such an address was ever prepared it never saw the light of day; the issuance of the Declaration made it unnecessary.

Although they postponed the vote on the resolution for independence for three weeks on June 10, Congress decided that they should have ready a formal announcement of this resolve when and if it was passed. To draft such an announcement they appointed a committee of five—Thomas Jefferson of Virginia, John Adams of Massachusetts, Benjamin Franklin of Pennsylvania, Roger Sherman of Connecticut and Robert Livingston of New York. Historians have speculated on why Jefferson, at thirty-three, the youngest and newest of its delegates, was selected to represent Virginia.

At the time Jefferson, unlike Franklin and Adams, had little national reputation. He had been a member of the House of Burgesses in Virginia and was a delegate to both sessions of the Second Continental Congress, but not yet a distinguished one. Many years later John Adams offered this explanation of Jefferson's appointment to the committee: "Mr. Jefferson had been now about a year a member of

Congress, but had attended his duty in the House a very small part of the time, and, when there, had never spoken in public. During the whole time I sat with him in Congress, I never heard him utter three sentences together. It will naturally be inquired how it happened that he was appointed on a committee of such importance. There were more reasons than one. Mr. Jefferson had the reputation of a masterly pen; he had been chosen a delegate in Virginia in consequency of a very handsome public paper which he had written for the House of Burgesses. . . . Another reason was that Mr. Richard Henry Lee was not loved by the most of his colleagues from Virginia, and Mr. Jefferson was set up to rival and supplant him. This could be done only by the pen, for Mr. Jefferson could stand no competition with him or anyone else in elocution and public debate."

This charge of friction within the Virginia delegation may have been a product of Adams' imagination. There is surely no evidence of any discord between Lee and Jefferson. Obviously, there should be a Virginian on the committee to draft a declaration of the resolution that Virginia had introduced, and Lee seemed to be the logical choice. He was the senior, he was the best known, and he had introduced the resolution. The reason he did not go on the committee is probably because he did not want to. His wife was ill in Virginia, and public business was pending there that required his attention. Two or three days after the committee was named he set out for Williamsburg, which he probably had intended to do all along.

In fact, Jefferson would rather have been in Williamsburg than in Philadelphia writing the Declaration of Independence. A convention was sitting back home to draft a state constitution, and both Lee and Jefferson undoubtedly considered this more vital than an announcement of even such an important national resolution as that for independence. Less than three weeks before his appointment to the committee Jefferson had written to a friend at the convention: "Should our Convention propose now to establish a form of government, perhaps it might be agreeable to recall for a short time their delegates [from the Continental Congress]. It is work of the most interesting nature and such as every individual would wish to have his voice in."

Since it was inevitable that there be a Virginian on the committee, Jefferson thus became the natural choice despite his youth. There was no doubt that his mind was prepared for the work at hand, and no other member of the Virginia delegation had any particular skill with the pen.

Another question that historians ponder is why Jefferson was chosen by the committee to write the Declaration. Adams later wrote that when Jefferson came to the Congress, he "brought with him a reputation for literature, science, and a happy talent of composition. Writings of his were handed about, remarkable for the peculiar felicity of expression." This was hindsight. To that time Jefferson's best-known composition was "A Summary View of the Rights of British America," a series of resolutions which he had sent to the burgesses, in 1774, as a proposed basis for instructions to the colony's delegates to the First Congress. This was the "handsome public paper," which Adams claimed was the reason for his choice as a delegate. Without Jefferson's knowledge, *Summary View* was printed in Williamsburg in booklet form and reprinted in Philadelphia and England, making it the most widely read of his writings during the revolution, except for the Declaration of Independence. *Summary View* established Jefferson among the liberals because, in it, he maintained that Parliament had no authority to legislate for the colonies; but, as a piece of writing, it was not "remarkable for the peculiar felicity of expression"—as Adams recalled many years later. On the whole, as a piece of prose it was not outstanding—certainly it did not compare with the Declaration or other of Jefferson's later writing, although it contained one sentence that, of itself, would justify immortality for the pamphlet:

> The God who gave us life gave us liberty at
> the same time; the hand of force may destroy,
> but cannot disjoin them.

Jefferson's only other important piece of writing, before the Declaration, was a draft of the "Declaration on the Necessity of Taking Up Arms," written during the first session of the Second Congress. This was too strong for the conservatives who controlled opinion at that time and it was considerably watered-down in revision by John Dickinson.

John Adams claimed that Jefferson was the chairman of the committee. "Upon this occasion I gave him my vote and did all in my power to procure the votes of others. I think he had one more vote than any other, and that placed him at the head of the committee. I had the next-highest number and that placed me second." This might be an explanation of why Jefferson did the writing. Forty-six years after the event, Adams, then an octogenarian, recalled a conversation with Jefferson on the subject of writing the Declaration that may or may not have taken place:

"The committee met, discussed the subject, and then

appointed Mr. Jefferson and me to make the draft; I suppose because we were the two highest on the list. The subcommittee met; Jefferson proposed to me to make the draft.

"I said, 'I will not; you shall do it.'

" 'Oh, no!'

" 'Why will you not?'

" 'You ought to do it.'

" 'I will not.'

" 'Why?'

" 'Reasons enough.'

" 'What can be your reasons?'

" 'Reason first. You are a Virginian and Virginia ought to appear at the head of this business. Reason second. I am obnoxious, suspected, and unpopular; you are very much other wise. Reason third. You can write ten times better than I can.'

" 'Well,' said Jefferson, 'if you are decided, I will do as well as I can.' "

Jefferson, by then also an octogenarian, did not agree with his old colleague as to the course of events in that memorable June. He wrote: "Mr. Adams' memory has led him into unquestionable error. At the age of eighty-eight, and forty-seven years after the transactions of independence, this is not wonderful. Nor should I, at the age of eighty, on the small advantage of that difference only, venture to oppose my memory to his, were it not supported by written notes, taken by myself at the moment and on the spot. . . . Now these details are quite incorrect. The committee of five met; so such thing as a subcommittee was proposed, but they unanimously pressed on myself alone to undertake the draft. I consented: I drew it."

Adams' reason for insisting that "Virginia ought to appear at the head of this business" was based on a policy that the Massachusetts delegates had adopted at the beginning of the Congress, on the advice, said Adams, of the Pennsylvania liberals. Massachusetts had a reputation for radicalism and any proposals by their delegates would be particularly suspect by the conservatives in the middle colonies and the south. The Pennsylvanians advised them, wrote Adams, to be: "very cautious; you must not come forward with any bold measures; you must not pretend to take the lead. You know Virginia is the most populous state in the Union. They are very proud of their ancient dominion, as they call it; they think they have a right to take the lead, and the Southern States, and Middle States, too, are too much disposed to yield it to them." A declaration written by a Massachusetts man would have less chance for universal approval than one written by a Virginian. Of course, Adams' third reason, "You can write ten times better than I can," was very valid. A declaration written in Adams' formal style would seem ponderous and dull compared to Jefferson's. Such a document would never have achieved immortality.

It was apparently never suggested that Franklin write the Declaration, which seems strange in view of the fact that he was far and away the best-known member of the committee nationally. He had represented Pennsylvania and other colonies in England. As a Pennsylvanian he was from the most conservative of the colonies; and he was the only man who had a national—in fact, a world-wide—reputation as a writer. Literary students have long speculated on what kind of a document the Declaration would have been if drafted by Franklin's pen, and wondered if it would have become sacred and immortal. It has been said, with a wit that would have delighted Franklin, that he probably would have put a joke in it if it had been committed to him. At the time he was suffering severely from gout. That, and his advanced age, may have had something to do with his staying in the background. At seventy he was almost old enough to be the grandfather of Jefferson.

According to the recollections of both Adams and Jefferson, the full committee met several times, probably in Franklin's home in view of his incapacity, and discussed the general form and content of the Declaration. Jefferson took the notes from these meetings to his lodgings in a brick building at the corner of Market and Seventh streets in Philadelphia. Here, he occupied a two-room suite, a bedroom and a parlor, that comprised the second floor. He worked in the parlor on a portable writing box—fourteen inches long, ten wide, and three deep—that had been made from his specifications and drawings by a carpenter. Perhaps the Virginian, as he wrote, had some premonition that the document he was drafting might have more lasting significance than merely an announcement of a Congressional resolution. In any event he kept the desk all his life. Less than a year before his death he gave it to his son-in-law, attaching to the underside a memorandum of the desk's pedigree: "Th. Jefferson gives this writing desk to Joseph Coolidge, Jr., as a memorial of affection. It was made from a drawing of his own, by Ben Randall, cabinetmaker of Philadelphia, with whom he first lodged on his arrival in that city in May, 1776, and is the identical one on which he wrote the Declaration of Independence. Politics, as well as religion, has its superstitions.

These gaining strength with time may, one day, give imaginary value to this relic, for its association with the birth of the great charter of our independence."

There is no record of how long it took Jefferson to write the Declaration. The work was encompassed between June 11 and June 28, when the document was submitted to Congress. At some time during this period he submitted what he called a rough draft to Franklin and Adams, probably twice. It is now apparent that he labored over the wording meticulously, before submitting the rough draft, and that this version was not the first draft.

The so-called rough draft was the earliest-known version of the Declaration until about twenty years ago, when there turned up, by chance, in the Library of Congress a scrap of paper which indicated that the rough draft was originally a clean copy of previous drafts. On this scrap is written, in Jefferson's hand, an acceptance of the resignation which Brigadier General John Sullivan tendered to Congress. But below this is a fragment of the Declaration of Independence, obviously an earlier version than the rough draft. Of the 156 words in the fragment, forty-three had been changed or corrected, indicating the extent to which Jefferson polished his composition, even before he made a draft to submit to anybody.

Jefferson had little trouble with his colleagues on the committee. The rough draft shows two fairly insignificant changes in Adams' hand, five in Franklin's. There are sixteen additional changes and three paragraphs in Jefferson's hand, which were added before the draft went to Congress. It cannot be determined whether these changes originated with

Jefferson or were suggested by other members of the committee.

The author did not fare so well in Congress, which spent the better part of three days going over the document, sentence by sentence, and making changes. In all there were eighty-six changes made, which eliminated 480 words. On the floor of Congress, Adams strenuously defended the Declaration as Jefferson had written it, while the author sat quietly by for propriety's sake—but he was not happy. Although all historians agree that most of the Congressional changes were improvements, the author writhed at what he later termed the "depredations" to his work. While Congress was tearing his precious document apart he was consoled by Franklin who, according to Jefferson, told him a story:

"I was sitting by Dr. Franklin, who perceived that I was not insensible to these mutilations. 'I have made it a rule,' said he, 'whenever in my power, to avoid becoming the draftsman of papers to be reviewed by a public body. I took my lesson from an incident which I will relate to you. When I was a journeyman printer, one of my companions, an apprentice hatter, having served his time was about to open shop for himself. His first concern was to have a handsome signboard with a proper inscription. He composed it in these words: "JOHN THOMPSON, HATTER, MAKES AND SELLS HATS FOR READY MONEY," with a figure of a hat subjoined. But he thought he would submit it to his friends for their amendments. The first he showed it to thought the word "HATTER" tautologous, because followed by the words, "MAKES HATS," which show he was a hatter. It was struck out. The next observed that the word "MAKES" might as well be omitted, because customers would not care who made the hats. If good and to their mind, they would buy, by whomever made. He struck it out. A third said he thought the words "FOR READY MONEY" were useless, as it was not the custom of the place to sell on credit. Everyone who purchased expected to pay. They were parted with and the inscription now stood: "JOHN THOMPSON SELLS HATS!" "Sells hats?" says his next friend. "Why, nobody will expect you to give them away. What then is the use of that word?" It was stricken out; and "HATS" followed it, the rather as there was one painted on the board. So his inscription was reduced ultimately to "JOHN THOMPSON" with the figure of a hat subjoined.' "

Jefferson's "Notes" on what happened on July 4, 1776, ended with: "The debates having taken up the greater parts of the second, third, and fourth of July were, in the evening of the last, closed [sic] the Declaration was reported to the committee, agreed to by the House, and signed by every member present except Mr. Dickinson." Actually, most students of the matter agree that nothing was signed on that day except by John Hancock, as president of Congress, and Charles Thomson, as secretary. Jefferson made some notes during the Congressional discussion of the document, and noted all the changes proposed by Congress on the rough draft, which he must have had before him. Later, he inserted a slip of paper into his original notes on which was written: "I took notes in my place while these things were going on, and at their close wrote them out in form and correctness." However, there is evidence that he edited and augmented his "Notes" many years later and it is possible that he inserted the comment on the signing at that time, and that his memory was faulty.

A controversy about the signing began in 1817 when Thomas McKean, a delegate from Delaware to the Second Congress, wrote a letter in which he said: "Now that I am on this subject, I will tell you some truths, not generally known. In the printed public *Journal of Congress* for 1776, Vol. 2, it would appear that the Declaration of Independence was signed on the fourth of July by the members, whose names are there inserted, but the fact is not so, for no person signed it on that day nor for many days after."

Opposed to this are letters of Franklin and Adams which state that the Declaration was signed on the fourth, but Franklin's was written ten years after the event and Adams' thirty-eight years later, and it is possible that their memories were faulty. Franklin wrote: "There is much rejoicing in town today, it being the anniversary of the Declaration of Independence, which we signed this day ten years, and thereby hazarded lives and fortunes." Adams wrote: "The final vote for independence, after the last debate, was passed on the second or third of July and the Declaration prepared and signed on the fourth. What are we to think of history when in less than forty years such diversities appear in the memories of living persons who were witnesses?"

But the evidence against a July 4 signing is overwhelming and includes the following points: (1) No copy with the original signature exists, nor is there a record of one, except the engrossed parchment copy that came later. (2) Neither the rough Journal of Congress, the corrected one, nor the "Secret Journal" mention a signing on that day. (3) The Declaration that was printed on the night of the fourth bears only the signatures of Hancock and Thomson. If the copy supplied to the printer had other signatures, why would the printer not include these as well as the names of the president and secretary? (4) On July 5, Samuel Chase wrote to John Adams from Annapolis, asking: "How shall I transmit to posterity that I gave my assent?"—to which Adams replied on July 9: "As soon as the American seal is prepared, I conjecture the Declaration will be subscribed by all the members which will give you the opportunity you wish for, of transfixing your name among the votaries of independence." No matter what he said thirty-eight years later, this letter written five days after the event mentions no signing on July 4. (5) on July 21, Elbridge Gerry, who was there on the fourth, wrote: "Pray subscribe for me ye Declaration of Independence if ye same is to be signed as proposed"—his letter implies that he had not previously signed. (6) The Journals of Congress note a resolution for the fourth that the Declaration should be "authenticated and printed"; a notation on the nineteenth of July states that it is to be "engrossed and signed."

A possible explanation for Jefferson's claim that the Declaration was signed on the fourth may be based on a reinterpretation of the sentence in which he made that statement. An unusual quirk in all of Jefferson's writing is that he usually started a sentence with a lower-case letter. The sentence in question reads: "the debates having taken up the greater part of the second, third, and fourth days of July were, in the evening of the last, closed [*sic*] the Declaration was reported by the committee, agreed to by the House, and signed by every member present except Mr. Dickinson." Obviously, punctuation is missing in this sentence; there should be either a period or a semicolon after the word "closed." In view of Jefferson's idiosyncracy of not using a capital to start a sentence, it might as well be the former as the latter. If the statement is thus divided into two senences, the words "in the evening of the last" may be construed to apply to the debates only. The statement "signed by every member" may apply to the later signing, which is authenticated by the *Journal of the Congress.*

The creditability of this section of Jefferson's "Notes" is also challenged by an obvious inaccuracy; the statement that the Declaration was signed by "every member present except Mr. Dickinson." The New York delegates did not vote for adopting the Declaration until they received permission from their state on July 15, and consequently could not have signed on July 4.

On the night of the fourth the Declaration was sent to a printer, Dunlap by name, who delivered printed copies the next day, one of which is wafered into the rough Journal of Congress, and is now in the Library of Congress. It has been said of this printed copy that the capitalization and punctuation followed "neither previous copies, nor reason, nor the custom of any age known to man." Dunlap may have been at fault in this, or the idiosyncracies may have been in the copy that he worked from. In any event, some allowance should be made for the pressure of time under which he worked.

There is one slight discrepancy between the printed copy and Jefferson's rough draft, which is also in the Congressional Library. The word "inalienable" in the draft became "unalienable" in the printed copy—and in all subsequent copies. This may have been a typographical error, or it may have been a change that Adams sneaked in when nobody was looking—the printing was supervised by members of the committee. Adams had made a copy in his own hand when Jefferson first submitted the document to him and in this copy the word is "unalienable." The Massachusetts lawyer thought that this was the proper spelling of the word (none of the Founding Fathers were very good spellers), and it is possible that he was merely correcting his colleague's spelling.

The parchment copy of the Declaration, which is now enshrined in the National Archives, was ordered by Congress on July 19, in a resolution that reads: "Resolved that the Declaration passed on the fourth be fairly engrossed on parchment with the title and style of 'The Unanimous Declaration of the Thirteen United States of America' and that the same be signed by every member of Congress." This engrossed copy was apparently received on August 2, for on that date the *Journal* states: "The Declaration of Independence being engrossed and compared at the table was signed." It obviously was not signed on that date by all who ultimately appended their signatures. One, Mathew Thornton of New Hampshire, did not join Congress until November 4. Lewis Morris of New York was away from June to September and could not have signed until after that time. Thomas McKean of Delaware was probably the last of the signers. Although he said in his old age that he had signed late in 1776, his name does not appear on a copy that was authenticated on January 17, 1777, so he probably signed after that time.

Much has been made about the fifty-six signers of the Declaration of Independence, starting with John Trumbull's famous painting. It surely will not lessen the merit of Trumbull's picture to point out that it is quite inaccurate, historically. The men whom he depicts as signing the Declaration in a group, whether it be on July 4 or August 2, were never in the same room at the same time. Some had left the Congress before others joined it. In fact, the signers of the Declaration of Independence bear only a partial relationship to the men who were involved in bringing it into being. Some time after it was adopted, a resolution was recorded in the "Secret Journal" of Congress: "To prevent traitors and spies from worming themselves amongst us no person shall have a seat in Congress until he should have signed the Declaration." This, rather than their views on independence or their participation in bringing it about, determined who signed the Declaration. Just how the requirement to sign would keep spies or traitors out of Congress is not clear. Perhaps it was felt that no renegade would be so bereft of honor as to sign the Declaration in order to hide his true purpose.

Approximately one quarter of the signers was not present when the Declaration was adopted. Only three of Pennsylvania's nine signers voted for the Declaration; five were not even members of Congress when it was adopted, nor was Thornton of New Hampshire. Oliver Wolcott, Philip Livingston, Lewis Morris, Richard Henry Lee, George Wythe, William Hooper, Samuel Chase, Charles Carroll, and possibly others were absent from Congress on July 4, and three Pennsylvanians who were members of Congress when the Declaration was adopted never did sign, nor did Robert Livingston, who was on the committee that drafted the Declaration. Believing its adoption inexpedient at the time he left Congress when New York accepted.

The fifty-six signers of the Declaration were in all re-

spects a diverse group of men. There were then no professional politicians; these men were all principally engaged in
some activity other than public service, prior to their membership in the Congress. Lawyers were more numerous than
representatives of any other occupation, but many of the
southern lawyers were planters who got their living from
the land rather than the law. There were four doctors and
one clergyman. Although the country was predominantly
agricultural, there were almost as many merchants as
planters and farmers, and a couple of the Pennsylvania delegates might be described as manufacturers. A few, like
Franklin, Jefferson, and Francis Hopkinson, had such a wide
range of interests and activities that they defy classification.

In age the signers ranged from twenty-six for Edward
Rutledge of South Carolina to seventy for Benjamin Franklin. Most of them were well to do, as they virtually had to
be in order to support their public work. A few, by the
standards of the times, were exceedingly wealthy. John
Hancock had inherited a large fortune. Robert Morris and
Philip Livingston were merchant princes. Charles Carroll,
a Maryland planter, was reputed to be the richest man in the
colonies.

Except for Hancock, who signed as President of the Congress, the delegates signed in groups, by colonies. Pennsylvania had the largest number of signers, nine; Rhode Island
the smallest, two. The larger and more populous colonies
had bigger delegations in the Congress, but each colony had
but one vote, regardless of size, so that Rhode Island and
Delaware carried as much weight in the balloting as Pennsylvania and Virginia.

The diversity of interests, background, and station in life

is evident from thumbnail biographies of the signers. If the names on the engrossed copy are read from left to right, Georgia comes first and the order proceeds from south to north. However, the names are here listed in the more customary north to south. The ages given are those at the time of signing.

New Hampshire's Josiah Bartlett, forty-seven, was a physician although he had many other interests. Before the Revolution he served as justice of the peace, provincial legislator, and colonel of militia. After the war he was a judge and, later, Governor of New Hampshire. He is reputed to have cast the first vote for the Declaration. He died at the age of sixty-six, leaving twelve children, three of whom, and seven grandsons, followed in his steps as physicians.

William Whipple, forty-seven, was a merchant in Portsmouth, New Hampshire, before he entered public service when the dispute with England became acute. Although he remained in the Congress until 1779, he left at intervals during the war to command New Hampshire troops, notably at the Battle of Saratoga, and is generally known as General Whipple. In later life he became a judge, a position that he held until his death at the age of fifty-six.

Mathew Thornton, sixty-two, was a physician who had been active in public life as a member of the New Hampshire legislature for twenty years, before he came to the Congress four months after the Declaration had been adopted. He remained in Congress only about a year and later served as a judge. (All three of New Hampshire's signers became judges, although none was a lawyer.) He died at the age of eighty-nine.

Samuel Adams, fifty-four, was the oldest of the five-man

Massachusetts delegation and, like the other four, a Harvard graduate. As a brewer and a tax collector, Adams was a failure, for he was ineffectual in all his private affairs. But no man did more, if as much, for the patriot cause before the Revolution. Among other things he organized the Sons of Liberty and the first Committee of Correspondence and was credited with the organization of the Boston Tea Party. He was completely and utterly dedicated to the cause of liberty, to the exclusion of every other interest, and after his service in Congress, which lasted until the end of the war, he lapsed into relative obscurity. His cousin John Adams described him as "a helpless object of compassion" in his last years, which may have been an exaggeration, but he was a "one cause" man and after that cause was won he never found another. He died at the age of eighty-one.

John Hancock, forty, was President of the Continental Congress. He has come down in history as a vain and flamboyant man, although his great service to the patriot cause prior to the Revolution cannot be questioned. He inherited a large fortune and, before he turned to public service, was active in real estate, shipping, and, if the truth be told, smuggling. Before coming to Congress he was a member of the Massachusetts General Court, as that colony's legislature was called and, according to Sam Adams, the town of Boston acquired his personal fortune when they elected him to public office. After the war he was Governor of Massachusetts for eleven years until his death at the age of fifty-six.

John Adams, forty-one, was a lawyer before he went to Congress. Because of his leadership during the debates on independence and the Declaration, he was dubbed "the Atlas of Independence." Despite his great qualities he was egotistical, impulsive, and often indiscreet. After his service in Congress he was commissioner to France with Jefferson and Franklin. With Franklin and Jay he negotiated the peace treaty with England and was later the first American minister to that country. After two terms as Vice-President to Washington he became the second President. His wife Abigail was one of the most extraordinary women of her time and together they founded an illustrious family. Son John Quincy became the sixth President, grandson Charles Francis was Ambassador to England during the Civil War, and great-grandsons Charles Francis, Henry, and Brooks were each distinguished in his own way. He died at the age of ninety-one on the fiftieth anniversary of the adoption of the Declaration.

Robert Treat Paine, forty-five, was a lawyer before he entered the first Continental Congress and a rather more moderate patriot than the other Massachusetts delegates, a signer of the Olive Branch Petition in the first session of the Second Congress. However, he finally strongly supported the Declaration. He later became first attorney-general of Massachusetts and a member of the state's supreme court. He died at the age of eighty-three.

Elbridge Gerry, thirty-two, was a well-to-do merchant. He was an early advocate of independence and a staunch supporter of the Declaration. After the war he had a checkered career. He remained in Congress until 1792 and was a member of the Constitutional Convention, although he refused to sign the Constitution. He switched from the Federalist to the Republican party because he considered the Federalists pro-British and, after several defeats, was elected Governor of Massachusetts. He was Vice-President under

Madison but alienated himself in his own state by staunchly supporting the War of 1812. He died while in office at the age of seventy-one, in a carriage en route to preside over the Senate.

Rhode Island's Stephen Hopkins, seventy, was, next to Franklin, the oldest signer. He was the nearest thing to a professional politician in the Congress, having held public office since the age of twenty-five, nine times as Governor of the colony, and also as chief justice. He was a prominent patriot before the first Congress and prevented the arrest of the burners of the *Gaspé*. He left Congress because of ill health in September, 1776, and, despite his lack of formal education, became the first chancellor of Rhode Island College. He died at the age of seventy-eight.

William Ellery, Rhode Island's other delegate, was forty-nine, a Harvard graduate and a lawyer. He had been in Congress only six weeks when the Declaration was adopted, but continued to serve in that body until 1786. It is said that Ellery, when most of the delegates signed the Declaration on August 2, took a position from which he could watch their faces. He reported that every one of them showed "undaunted resolution." After his retirement from Congress, President Washington appointed him collector of customs for the port of Newport, a position which he held for thirty years until his death at the age of ninety-three.

Connecticut's Roger Sherman, fifty-five, was a plain man of humble origin, with little formal education, although, as an avid reader, he was a well-informed individual. He started as a cobbler, acquired land, and became a lawyer and a merchant. He was noted for the number of public offices that he held concurrently, among others, membership on the Connecticut legislature for twenty years and judge of the superior court. Despite his lack of education, he was associated with Yale, which gave him an honorary M.A. He served in both Congresses, where he had a reputation of being "cunning as the Devil," and was a member of the committee that drafted the Declaration, although there is no evidence of what, if anything, he contributed to it. But there is no question of his later contribution to the Constitutional Convention, where he introduced what has become known as the "Great Compromise." He was the only man known to have signed the Association of 1774, in the First Congress, the Declaration of Independence, the Articles of Confederation, and the Constitution of the United States. After the Constitution was adopted he served a term in the House of Representatives and was in the Senate when he died at the age of seventy-two.

Oliver Wolcott, fifty, the son of a colonial governor, was a Yale graduate and a lawyer. Because of illness he left Congress in June, 1776, and was not involved in the adoption of the Declaration, which he signed after his return to Philadelphia in October. Meanwhile, he had brought from New York to his home town of Litchfield the equestrian statue of George III, which he melted down to make bullets. He remained a member of Congress until the end of the war, but spent much time in the field as a brigadier and then as a major general. After the war he was a commissioner to the Six Nations to sign the Treaty of Fort Stanwix, Lieutenant Governor and then Governor of Connecticut, in which office he died at the age of seventy-one.

William Williams, forty-five, had studied theology at Harvard but, after serving in the French and Indian War, he became a businessman in Lebanon, Connecticut, where he was also selectman and town clerk. He was supposed to replace Wolcott in Congress when that member left to take the field and probably arrived in Philadelphia in time to vote for the Declaration. After a couple of years in Congress he left to engage in public work in his state as a member of the Governor's council and as a local judge. He died at the age of eighty.

Samuel Huntington, forty-five, was the son of a farmer who, with little education, had become apprenticed to a cooper. He studied law on his own and became a member of the upper house of the state legislature and a judge of the superior court before he came to the Congress in 1775. He served in the Congress for a decade and, for two years, was its president. After the war he became Governor of Connecticut for a dozen years and, in 1788, he received two electoral votes in the presidential contest. He died at the age of sixty-five.

New York's Francis Lewis, sixty-three, was a retired merchant. A self-made man who had been orphaned as a child, he retired from business in his fifties and entered public life when the dispute with Britain became acute. He was generally inactive in the Continental Congress and was described as one of two members who "never quit their chairs." Because of the instructions from his colony he, with the other New York delegates, was unable to vote for the adoption of the Declaration on July 4. He stayed in Congress until 1779, did some public service for a couple of years thereafter, and then retired completely at the age of sixty-eight. He was nearly ninety when he died in 1802.

Philip Livingston, sixty-one, was a Yale graduate and a

member of one of the great manorial families of New York who added to inherited wealth by importing and other mercantile ventures. Although he sponsored the patriot cause from the time of the Stamp Act and strongly opposed Parliament's right to tax the colonies, he was known as a moderate who opposed the riotous acts of the Sons of Liberty. Before serving in the Congress he had helped to organize King's College (now Columbia University) and the New York Society Library, and was a member of the provincial legislature. He was not present during the debates on the Declaration but signed it in August. The name Livingston is confusing in that there were three members of that family in the Second Congress. William, Philip's brother, left in June, 1776, to command New Jersey troops. Robert, his cousin, was on the committee to draft the Declaration but neither voted for it nor signed it. Philip was still a member of the Congress when he died in 1778, at the age of sixty-two.

Lewis Morris, fifty, was also a Yale graduate and a member of New York's landed gentry. His vocation was that of a country gentleman. As a member of the colony's assembly he had condemned British policy before coming to the Congress. In June, 1776, he left Congress to command Westchester County militia with the rank of brigadier general, but saw little or no active service. He was not present in Congress when the Declaration was adopted, but signed it after he got back to Philadelphia in September. He died at the age of seventy-one.

William Floyd, forty-two, was another country gentleman who inherited a large fortune, although he had relatively little schooling. He held the rank of major general of militia before he went to the First and the Second Continental Congress, where he took no part in debates, although, said another member, he always voted with "the zealous friends of liberty and independence." He continued to serve in Congress throughout the war and was later a state senator and a member of Congress after the adoption of the Constitution. He was ruined financially by the Revolution and retired to upstate New York, where he died in his eighty-seventh year.

The five-man New Jersey delegation was unusual in that they were all fledgling members of Congress when the Declaration came up for adoption. Benjamin Franklin's son William was Royal Governor of New Jersey until he was ousted in June, 1776. At the same time, the provincial legislature elected a fresh slate of delegates to the Continental Congress and empowered them to vote for independence. John Adams dubbed this reinforcement to the ranks of the liberals "five independent souls."

John Hart, sixty-five, was a farmer and mill owner with little schooling. He was a member of his colony's assembly when elected to the Congress. His lands were laid waste by the British and he was, for a time, a fugitive before he died in 1779 at the age of sixty-eight.

John Witherspoon, fifty-four, was a minister and President of the College of New Jersey (now Princeton), where James Madison was among his pupils. Born in Scotland, he had become an American only six or seven years before the Declaration and generally disapproved of clergymen participating in politics. However, he accepted his election to the Congress and, on July 2, made an impassioned speech for independence, saying that the country was, "not only ripe

for the measure, but in danger of rotting for the want of it."
He remained in Congress until 1782, where his activities on
the Committee of Secret Correspondence (the forerunner
of the Department of State) were of great value. For a
dozen years after the war, he labored at restoring the college
and in organizing the Presbyterian Church in the United
States, for which he was chiefly responsible. He died at the
age of seventy-two.

Richard Stockton, forty-five, was a Princeton graduate
and a lawyer who was influential in the affairs of his alma
mater. He was a justice of the supreme court of New Jersey
when elected to the Congress. When the British overran
New Jersey in 1776, he got his family to safety but was
himself captured. The conditions of his captivity wrecked
his health and after his exchange he was an invalid until his
death in 1781 at the age of fifty-one.

Abraham Clark, fifty, was a poor man with but a smattering of education. He was known as "The Poor Man's Coun-
sellor," although there is no record that he was ever admitted to the bar. He worked as a surveyor, was sheriff of
Essex County and clerk of his colony's assembly before
coming to Congress. He stayed in Congress for several years
and thereafter was active in his state's affairs, serving in the
Second and Third Congresses under the Constitution. He
died at the age of sixty-nine.

Francis Hopkinson, thirty-eight, was the first graduate of
the College of Philadelphia (later the University of Pennsylvania). His interests were so broad that he is difficult to
classify. He practiced law, but he was also a composer, an
outstanding performer on the harpsichord, and a minor in-
ventor. He was also something of an artist and, during the

tedious debates of Congress, relieved his boredom by drawing caricatures of his colleagues. He was a member of the Governor's Council when elected to the Congress. During the war he was chairman of the Continental Navy Board and is said to have designed the American flag in 1777. After the war he continued in public work, although now in Pennsylvania, but was probably more interested in scientific and philosophical correspondence with Jefferson, Franklin, and David Rittenhouse. President Washington appointed him judge of the Federal Court in Pennsylvania, a position which he held until his death at the age of fifty-four.

It is impossible to write a thumbnail biography of the Declaration's oldest signer, Pennsylvania's Benjamin Franklin. Merely to list his interests, accomplishments, and activities would take far more space than that provided by the largest thumb. With but a smattering of education, he had risen to be the most eminent writer, philosopher, scientist, statesman, and diplomat in the colonies before he joined Congress. He had also founded the first circulating library in America, the American Philosophical Society, the academy that became the University of Pennsylvania, laid the foundation for the science of electricity, written the famous *Sayings of Poor Richard,* and been the deputy postmaster general of the colonies. During the seventeen years before 1775, he had spent most of his time in England as agent for several colonies. Later, he would go to France to make the treaty which made that country an ally, and negotiate the treaty of peace with Great Britain. He was the only Founding Father to sign all four of the documents that were of importance in creating the nation: The Declaration of Independence, the Treaty with France, the Treaty of Peace, and the Constitution. He died in 1790 at the age of eighty-four.

John Morton, approximately fifty-two, was a plain farmer who had served in the Pennsylvania legislature and on the bench for several years before coming to Congress. He had no formal education, but was well taught at home by his stepfather. He was a member of both Congresses and he, Franklin, and Wilson were the only liberals among Pennsylvania's nine-man delegation at the time the Declaration was adopted, and the only three who both voted for it and signed it. He was the first of the signers to die, in April, 1777, less than ten months after the signing.

James Wilson, thirty-three, was a Scottish-born lawyer, educated at St. Andrews, and was one of the first to deny all authority of Parliament. A pamphlet that he wrote on the subject anticipated the later British Commonwealth of autonomous states, with allegiance to the King the only connection with the Empire. He was a moderate among the Liberals, advocating as late as June, 1776, the postponement of independence. However, on July 2, he supported Franklin and John Morton to give a majority for independence of the five Pennsylvania delegates who were then present. In a sense, it might be said that his was the vote that decided independence, for had he voted in line with his opinion in June, Pennsylvania would not have supported the resolution. He left Congress in 1777 but returned to public life in time to play a commanding role in the Constitutional Convention, where he was said to be second in influence only to James Madison. He later became the first associate justice of the United States Supreme Court and was responsible for a decision that was the basis of the Eleventh Amendment to the Constitution, which denies citizens of one state the right to sue another state in federal court. An inveterate land speculator, Wilson said that he was "hunted like a wild beast" by his creditors, before he died, in 1798, at the age of fifty-five.

Robert Morris, forty-three, was born in Liverpool, came to America at the age of thirteen, with but slight schooling. He shortly became a partner in the mercantile firm of Willing, Morris and Co. His partner, Willing, was also a member of the Pennsylvania delegation in early July, but voted against the Declaration and never signed it. Morris, who opposed the timing of the Declaration, not the act itself, absented himself during the voting but later signed. Morris' great contribution to the cause was in the procurement and handling of money; he has been called the "financier of the revolution," a position in which he kept the Continental treasury from foundering on several occasions, although he handled his position with such a high hand that he was called "the dictator." He was one of the first senators from Pennsylvania after the Constitution was adopted and, shortly thereafter, he lost his personal fortune in land speculation. He spent three and one half years in prison for debt and the last five years of his life in obscurity, until he died at the age of seventy-two.

The remaining five delegates from Pennsylvania were elected late in July, 1776, to replace the conservatives and, therefore, had nothing to do with the adoption of the resolution. However, they signed it on August 2.

George Taylor, sixty, was born in Northern Ireland and might be termed a manufacturer, since he operated an iron furnace. His political activities before going to Congress were limited to a short term in the colonial assembly. He served less than a year in Congress, where he was relatively inactive. Later, he was elected to the Supreme Executive Council of his state but retired after a few weeks because of ill health. He died in 1781 at the age of sixty-five.

James Smith, fifty-seven, was, like his colleague Taylor, born in Northern Ireland and came to America at the age of ten. He was a lawyer who was also engaged in the iron business. He was a staunch advocate of colonial rights from the western part of the state and a member of several congresses and conventions before coming to the Congress. His service in Congress was inconspicuous until he left in 1778. He later held several state posts until he died at the age of about eighty-seven.

George Ross, forty-six, was a lawyer and a member of the provisional assembly before he came to Congress, where he did nothing memorable except to sign the Declaration, until he withdrew in 1777. He later became a judge of the admiralty court in Pennsylvania. He died in 1779 at the age of forty-nine.

George Clymer, thirty-seven, was a Philadelphia merchant and a patriot to the point that, in 1776, he unwisely exchanged all of his specie for Continental currency. After the war he was a member of the Pennsylvania assembly, the Constitutional Convention, and the first Congress under the Constitution. He died at the age of seventy-three.

Benjamin Rush, thirty-one, was a Princeton graduate and America's most famous physician, although he had many other interests. As a leading light in the American Philosophical Society, he was a close friend of Jefferson and Franklin, and a particular friend of John Adams. It was he who, years later, healed the ten-year breech in the relationship between Adams and Jefferson. In 1777 he left Congress to become surgeon-general of the armies. An impulsive man—he once described prudence as "a rascally virtue"—Rush made some intemperate remarks about Washington, which led to his being wrongfully accused of participation in the "Conway Cabal" against the general. After the war he crusaded against slavery, tobacco, alcohol, and a classical education; he corresponded omnivorously, particularly with his friends Jefferson and Adams, some of whose best letters were in reply to those from the doctor. When finally published in the mid-twentieth century, his correspondence threw much light on the social and scientific history of his times and on his fellow patriots of the Revolution. He died in 1813 at the age of sixty-eight.

Delaware's Caesar Rodney, forty-eight, was a Maryland planter who entered public life early through membership in his colony's assembly and as a brigadier general of militia. He left Congress to take the field and was for a time in command of the post at Trenton. He was elected Governor of Delaware in 1778, a post in which he served during a large part of the Revolution. His greatest claim to fame is his gallop from Wilmington to Philadelphia on the night of July 3, to record his colony's vote for independence. He died in 1784 at the age of fifty-six.

George Read, forty-three, was a lawyer, a member of the Delaware assembly, and both Congresses. He was the Delaware delegate who opposed independence on July 2, although he later signed the Declaration and loyally supported it. He was Governor of his state before Rodney and later a member of the Constitutional Convention, and led Delaware to ratify that document first among the states. He was a Senator from Delaware from the beginning of the new government until 1798, when he became chief justice of his state. He died in 1798 at the age of sixty-five.

Thomas McKean, forty-two, was a lawyer, a perennial member of the Delaware assembly since his youth, and a noted liberal. He remained in the Congress until the end of the war, for a short time was Governor of Delaware and, at the same time, chief justice of Pennsylvania. Finally he was Governor of Pennsylvania. He died in 1817 at the age of eighty-three.

Maryland's Charles Carroll of Carrollton, thirty-nine, was the only Catholic signer and the only millionaire among the group. The "of Carrollton" was customarily part of his signature because there were so many Charles Carrolls in Maryland, all related. He had studied law in Paris and London but was principally a planter. He was an active patriot before going to Congress, although he held no public office. Early in 1776 he was sent to Canada with Franklin and Samuel Chase on a fruitless errand to try to win that colony over to the rebellion. He remained in Congress for a couple of years and later served in the Maryland senate and the United States Senate. He was the last of the signers to die. None of the others knew any mode of land transport except the horse; Carroll laid the cornerstone of the Baltimore and Ohio Railroad, before he died in 1832 at the age of ninety-five.

William Pica, thirty-six, was a lawyer and a graduate of the College of Philadelphia (later the University of Pennsylvania). A leading patriot in Maryland, he was a member of both Congresses, staying until 1779. He was later Governor of Maryland and finally a United States district judge, a post that he held until his death in 1799 at the age of fifty-nine.

Samuel Chase, thirty-five, was a lawyer with a long record of service in the Maryland assembly. As the most aggressive anti-British leader in his colony, he was a delegate to both Congresses. He was chiefly responsible for swinging Maryland into the independence camp, in June, 1776, and carried the assembly's instructions to that effect to Philadelphia. While in Congress he was charged by the press with using inside information to speculate in flour. His business ventures after the war left him insolvent. He opposed the Constitution in 1787, then became a Federalist and supported it to the extent that President Washington appointed him an associate justice of the Supreme Court, where he had such a stormy career that he was impeached, but acquitted, during Jefferson's administration. He remained on the court until his death in 1811 at the age of seventy.

Thomas Stone, thirty-three, was a lawyer with no record of public service until he entered Congress, in 1775, as the most moderate of the Maryland delegates. He seldom spoke either in Congress or in the Maryland legislature, of which he was later a member. He died in 1787 at the age of forty-four.

Richard Henry Lee, forty-five, was the ranking member of Virginia's outstanding seven-man delegation. As a member of a wealthy family of planters he was educated abroad and became a member of the House of Burgesses as a matter of course, where he early became associated with the radical faction of which Patrick Henry was the leader. Like Henry, he was a noted orator. Although he introduced the resolution for independence, he did not stay in Philadelphia to vote for it or for the Declaration, but he returned to sign the document in August. Somewhat later he became involved in a controversy between his brother Arthur and Silas Deane, who had preceded Franklin as commissioner to Paris, France, as a result of which he became very unpopular at home. He strongly opposed the Constitution, in 1787, and his *Letters of a Federal Farmer* became something of a bible to the opposition. He served briefly in the first United States Senate before he died in 1794 at the age of sixty-three.

As with Franklin, it is impossible to capsulize Thomas Jefferson who, next to the old sage, was the most versatile man of his era; although at the time he signed the Declaration, at the age of thirty-three, his full stature was not apparent. He was a graduate of William and Mary College, a planter, a lawyer, and a member of the House of Burgesses, who had some facility with the pen. He had already, with that pen, led several liberal crusades in Virginia, including the abolition of entails, the disestablishment of the church, a revision of the legal code, and forward-looking proposals on education. He was Governor of Virginia during much of the war and later succeeded Franklin as Ambassador to France before joining Washington's cabinet as the first Secretary of State. He was Vice-President under Adams and the leader of the Republican-Democrat party, which ousted the Federalists by electing him to the Presidency in 1801. He was the greatest champion of individual human rights, a strong proponent of education, and achieved much in invention, agriculture, science, and architecture, among other fields. He died, virtually bankrupt, at the age of eighty-three, on the same day as John Adams, the fiftieth anniversary of the Declaration.

Benjamin Harrison, fifty, was a graduate of William and Mary, a planter, and long-time member of the House of Burgesses before he went to the first Continental Congress. When Congress resolved itself into a committee of the whole he replaced John Hancock as chairman and presided over the debates on the Declaration. After leaving Congress in 1778, he spent the rest of his life holding office in Virginia. He was the principal opponent of the adoption of the Constitution without the inclusion of a Bill of Rights before, rather than after, its ratification. He died in 1791 at the age of sixty-five.

George Wythe, fifty, was a graduate of William and Mary, a lawyer who taught that profession to Jefferson, and a member of the House of Burgesses. In 1778 he became judge in Virginia's high court of chancery and the next year he joined the faculty of William and Mary, to become the first professor of law in an American college. His death, at the age of eighty, was caused by drinking coffee which his nephew and principal beneficiary had laced with arsenic.

Francis Lightfoot Lee, forty-two, was the younger brother of Richard Henry Lee. He, too, was a planter, a member of the House of Burgesses from the age of twenty-four, and an ardent patriot, although, unlike his brother, he seldom spoke on the subject. He remained in Congress until 1779 and thereafter served briefly in the Virginia legislature before an early retirement. He died in 1797 at the age of sixty-three.

Carter Braxton, forty, was a planter, a graduate of William and Mary, and a long-time member of the House of Burgesses. On the subject of independence he was the most moderate of his colony's delegation. When Virginia cut its delegation to Congress from seven to five in the late summer of 1776, he was not re-elected, but was a member of the state's General Assembly for most of the rest of his life. The war ruined him financially and during his last years he lived in obscurity in Richmond, where he died in 1797 at the age of sixty-one.

Thomas Nelson, Jr., thirty-seven, was a merchant planter, educated at Cambridge in England, and a friend of Jefferson's when the latter was a student at William and Mary in his late teens. He was the only member of the Virginia Delegation who was not also a member of the House of Burgesses. Nelson left Congress in 1777 to take the field as a brigadier general, and in 1781 succeeded Jefferson as Governor when the state was overrun by the British. He commanded troops at Yorktown and, according to legend, pleaded with Washington to shell his own home, which Cornwallis was using as headquarters. Both Nelson's health and fortune were ruined by the war and at its end he retired to a small estate, where he died in 1789 at the age of sixty.

North Carolina's Joseph Hewes, forty-six, was a prosperous merchant and, initially, a Quaker. He was a member of the provincial assembly before attending both the first and second Congresses. He was a moderate patriot who did not approve of an open breach with the mother country until advice from his state convinced him that public opinion favored it. As chairman of the Marine Committee in Congress he was virtually the first Secretary of the Navy. He failed of re-election in 1777 but returned briefly to Congress in 1779, where he died at the age of forty-nine.

John Penn, thirty-six, was a lawyer and member of North Carolina's provincial congress before coming to the Congress. He seldom spoke in Congress, except to whisper to the member sitting next to him, but remained in that body until 1780. After some slight public service back home he retired because of ill health and died in 1788 at the age of forty-eight.

William Hooper, thirty-four, was a graduate of Harvard, a lawyer and a member of the provincial congress before serving in both Congresses. He was absent when the Declaration was adopted, but later signed it. After the war he served in the North Carolina legislature for five years, without particular distinction. Like many of the patriots his personal fortunes were ruined by the war. He died in 1790 at the age of forty-eight.

South Carolina's Arthur Middleton, thirty-four, was a lawyer-planter, educated in England, and renowned as a classic scholar who read Latin and Greek for relief from public affairs. As a member of his colony's provincial assembly he was regarded as the leader of the extreme liberals before he replaced his father in Congress sometime after May of 1776. It is not certain that he was present at the adoption of the Declaration. As an officer of militia he was imprisoned by the British after the fall of Charlestown, as were two of the other South Carolina signers, Heyward and Rutledge. He apparently did not re-enter public life after the war. He died in 1787 at the age of forty-five.

Thomas Heyward, Jr., thirty, was a lawyer-planter who did not go to Congress until a provisional government had been set up in South Carolina in the spring of 1776; his position on the subject of independence before July 2 is not certain, although Dr. Rush described him as a "firm republican." He remained in Congress until 1778 and served as an artillery officer in the south before his capture at Charlestown. He was in the legislature and on the bench in his home state after the war but soon retired to devote himself to his plantation, where he died in 1809 at the age of sixty-three.

Edward Rutledge, twenty-six, was the youngest signer. He was educated in England and, like so many of his southern colleagues, was a lawyer-planter. He was appointed to the first Congress when only twenty-four, and was a moderate independent who is generally considered as being responsible for the postponement of the vote on independence from June 7 to July. However, he is also given the major credit for the decision of South Carolina's delegation to go along with the majority on July 2. Rutledge left the Congress in the fall of 1776 and served with his state's troops until captured. He was later Governor of his state but died in 1800, at the age of fifty, before completing his term.

Thomas Lynch, Jr., twenty-seven, was, like Middleton, a substitute for his father in Congress. He was educated at Eton and Cambridge and became a lawyer-planter who was elected to local public office in his early twenties. In ill health, he remained in Congress but a few months after the signing. He was lost at sea on a voyage to the West Indies in 1779, when he was but thirty years of age.

Georgia's Lyman Hall, fifty-two, was one of the most radical patriots in that remote colony, where loyalist sentiment was so strong that it was virtually a British outpost. He was a Yale graduate who, after spending some years as a minister, became a physician and a rice planter. Hall entered the Congress in 1775 and remained until 1780. After the war he returned to Savannah to practice medicine and later became Governor of the state. He died in 1790 at the age of sixty-six.

Button Gwinnett, forty-one, was born in England. He was first a merchant in Savannah and then a planter and a member of the provincial assembly. He did not arrive in Philadelphia until May, and returned to Georgia shortly after signing the Declaration. Later he became Governor of Georgia for a couple of months until he became embroiled in a controversy with General Lachlan McIntosh, arising out of his criticism of an unsuccessful military expedition into Florida. McIntosh challenged Gwinnett to a duel, in which the latter received a wound from which he died a few days later on May 16, 1777, at the age of forty-two. Gwinnett's name is the first on the engrossed copy of the Declaration, after President Hancock's. His main contemporary fame is based upon the fact that his signature is the rarest and, therefore, the most valuable of any of the signers.

George Walton, thirty-five, a lawyer, was an orphan who had been apprenticed to a carpenter and was largely self-taught. He did not reach Philadelphia until late in May, shortly after his two colleagues. Because of Georgia's remoteness, her delegates were uninstructed, so that they were able to vote their personal convictions; this is fortunate because the extreme loyalist sentiment in that colony makes it unlikely that the delegates would have been instructed to vote for independence. He was in Congress during most of the war, although he commanded militia at the siege of Savannah in 1778, where he was wounded, captured, and exchanged. Later he was chief justice of the state,

Governor, and finally United States Senator. He died in 1804 at the age of sixty-three.

Although the signers are celebrated as the champions of liberty, it is a fact that several of them had nothing to do with the passage of the resolution for independence on the adoption of the Declaration; it may be true, as John Adams believed, that some of them signed unwillingly. When asked about it years later, he said, "When finally accepted, all those who had voted against independence now declared they would sign it and support it. . . . As I could not see into their hearts, it would be hard for me to say that they did not approve it. But as far as I could penetrate the intricate foldings of their souls, I then believed, and since then have not altered my opinion, that there were several who signed with regret and several others with many doubts." The regret and doubt, if such existed—and they probably did—were, in some cases, based on the individual's political convictions or philosophy; in others, on the very real danger involved. Had the colonies lost, the signers might well have been proscribed and tried for treason. As it was, many of the wealthier ones suffered serious economic loss as a result of the war.

Several legends about the signing have come down in history; it would be amazing if this were not so in connection with such a historic event. The most famed is a saying attributed to Franklin. When Hancock observed, "We must be unanimous; there must be no pulling different ways; we must all hang together," Franklin is supposed to have replied, "Yes, we must all hang together, or most assuredly we will all hang separately." This saying first appeared about half a century after Franklin's death and, although it would be in character for the old sage, it is probable that it would have been quoted earlier if he really had said it.

Less known is the supposed conversation between Benjamin Harrison of Virginia, a very obese gentleman, and Elbridge Gerry of Massachusetts, a virtual skeleton. Harrison is supposed to have said to Gerry, when he signed: "When the hanging scene comes to be exhibited, my friend, I shall have all the advantage over you . . . with me it will be over in a minute. But you, you'll be dancing on air for an hour after I'm gone." The thought of possible punishment was probably in the minds of many. Charles Carroll is supposed to have said that he signed "of Carrollton," after his name, so that when the British came for him they would get the right Carroll; although, in fact, Carroll habitually signed his name this way. John Hancock is supposed to have said he signed his name so boldly so that John Bull could read it without spectacles, and could double the reward on his head. There had been a reward offered for the capture of Hancock and Adams since before the Battles of Lexington and Concord; warning them was the primary purpose of Paul Revere's ride. Hancock's defiance at the signing created a lasting figure of speech. To this day, signing one's "John Hancock" is synonomous for affixing a signature.

Although anyone who was interested would have little trouble in learning the names of the signers, they were not widely publicized, except for that of Hancock, which was on the printed document, until January 18, 1777. On that date Congress resolved that an authenticated copy of the Declaration, with the names of those who had subscribed to it, should be printed and sent to each of the states. More than six months elapsed between the time the Declaration was adopted and the time that it was officially published, although copies of the Dunlap printing had been previously sent to the assemblies, conventions, and committees or councils of safety, and the commanding officers of the Continental troops. A resolution of Congress provided that it be proclaimed in each of the United States and at the head of the Army.

Although some of the signers became major heroes of American history and two of them became United States Presidents, most of them sank to relative obscurity back in their own states. But probably even those who may have signed with regret or doubt ultimately came to agree with the deathbed message that John Morton left for his family: "Tell them that they shall live to see the hour when they shall acknowledge it to be the most glorious service I ever rendered my country." Certainly, fifty years later, both John Adams and Thomas Jefferson felt that signing the Declaration of Independence was the most important act of their lives.

The Drafts of the Declaration

One who enjoys hairsplitting might make the point that there is really no such thing as "The Declaration of Independence." There are what might be called three official versions of the document and none of them bear that title.

The earliest version is the rough draft, in Jefferson's hand, which is in the Library of Congress. Jefferson called his work: "A Declaration by the Representatives of the UNITED STATES OF AMERICA in General Congress Assembled."

The next copy in point of time is that which Dunlap printed on the night of July 4, and which is now in the *Journal of Congress*, in the Congressional Library. This is titled: "IN CONGRESS, JULY 4th, 1776. A DECLARATION By the Representatives of the UNITED STATES OF AMERICA IN GENERAL CONGRESS Assembled."

The third is the engrossed parchment copy which was signed, starting on August 2, and which is now on display in the National Archives. This is titled: "In CONGRESS, July 4th, 1776. The unanimous Declaration of the thirteen united STATES OF AMERICA." It will be noted that the word "Independence" does not appear in any of the titles, although it is possible that Jefferson started to write "A Declaration of Independence," because the rough draft shows that the word "of" was originally written after the "Declaration," and "by" was then substituted.

Two things on which the documents all agree is that it is a declaration and that it is made by the "United States." This is the first time that such a name for the colonies was officially used, although the thinking as to the relative importance of "States" and "united," at the time, may be inferred from the fact that the former word is capitalized and the latter is in lower case in the parchment copy. Also, in the parchment copy, the word "unanimous" is added—a word that could not be used in the title of the printed copy because New York had not yet signified its approval.

The famed parchment copy is said to have been made by one, Timothy Matlack, and the writing, which was of the type customarily used in formal documents, made a pleasing over-all appearance at a sacrifice of readability. There are no paragraphs, as such. Paragraphing is indicated by dashes. The use of lower-case lettering for the word "united," although it was significant of opinion toward union at the time, was probably occasioned by the desire to get the entire title on one line.

Other early texts of the Declaration include a copy, in the hand of Charles Thomson, in the so-called corrected

Journal of Congress, now in the Library of Congress; a copy made by John Adams, apparently on the first occasion that Jefferson submitted it to him, now in the Adams Family Papers; a copy made by Jefferson that he sent to Richard Henry Lee, now in the American Philosophical Society; another copy made by Jefferson and sent to George Wythe, now in the New York Public Library; an incomplete copy made by Jefferson and sent to George Pendleton, now in the Massachusetts Historical Society; another Jefferson copy that was sent to James Madison, which is with the Madison Papers in the Library of Congress.

But none of these official versions or early copies is what might be termed the "original" of the Declaration: the copy that the committee submitted to the Congress. Jefferson wrote that after submitting the document in the form of the rough draft to Adams and Franklin, he made "a fair copy, reported it to the committee, and from them unaltered to Congress." No such copy exists and, except for this statement of Jefferson's, there is nowhere else a reference to it.

One point of view has it that there never was a fair copy, that Jefferson's memory was at fault in the matter, and that the rough draft was the copy submitted to Congress. This viewpoint is inferentially endorsed by a letter from John Adams, in which he says: "We were all in haste; Congress was impatient and the instrument was reported, I believe, in Jefferson's hand as he first drew it." But logic commands that there must have been a fair copy, for two simple reasons. All of Congress' changes were noted by Jefferson in the rough draft. He either had it before him and made the changes as they were decided upon, or later conformed it to some other copy. Some copy was provided to Dunlap from which to set the document, and it is not credible that this was the rough draft, which is so interlined with corrections that it virtually cannot be read without the aid of a glass. No compositor could set type from it in the time allowed. Also, Dunlap's version contains the names of Hancock and Thomson, which must have been on the copy that he received and are not on the rough draft.

There surely was a fair copy of the Declaration as Jefferson wrote it, with his subsequent additions and the few changes of Adams and Franklin. This, Thomson undoubtedly had before him while the document was debated, and noted thereon the changes of Congress before it was signed by Hancock and himself and sent to Dunlap. The interesting question is: What happened to it? The most likely answer is that it never came back from the printer—some unknown journeyman or printer's devil probably threw away the original of the Declaration of Independence, or took it home as a souvenir where, perhaps, it was used to start a fire. The absence of this copy is another indication that the Declaration was not signed on the fourth. Charles Thomson was meticulous about saving the official documents of the Congress; surely a copy that had been formally signed by the members would have been guarded more carefully.

Through a comparison of the copy made by Adams—presumably on the first submission to him, since it contains only one of his two changes and two of Franklin's five—it is possible to reconstruct the Declaration as Jefferson wrote it, and to compare it with the document as Congress adopted it, in the form of the copy printed by Dunlap. In the columns below, the rough draft as it probably was when

Jefferson first submitted it to Franklin is on the left; the copy printed by Dunlap is on the right:

A Declaration by the Representatives of the UNITED STATES OF AMERICA, in GENERAL Congress assembled.

When in the course of human events it becomes necessary for a people to advance from that subordination in which they have hitherto remained, & to assume among the powers of the earth the equal and independent station to which the laws of nature & of nature's god entitle them, a decent respect to the opinions of mankind requires that they should declare the causes which impel them to the change.

We hold these truths to be
self-evident
sacred and undeniable; that all men are created equal & independent; that from that equal creation they derive in rights inherent & inalienable, among which are the preservation of life, & liberty, & the pursuit of happiness; that to secure these ends, governments are instituted among men, deriving their just powers from the consent of the governed; that whenever any form of government shall be-

In CONGRESS, July 4, 1776
A DECLARATION
By the REPRESENTATIVES of the UNITED STATES OF AMERICA,
In GENERAL CONGRESS assembled.

When in the Course of human Events, it becomes necessary for one People to dissolve the Political Bands which have connected them with another, and to assume among the Powers of the Earth, the separate and equal Station to which the Laws of Nature and of Nature's God entitle them, a decent Respect to the Opinions of Mankind requires that they should declare the causes which impel them to the Separation.

We hold these Truths to be self evident, that all Men are created equal, that they are endowed by their Creator with certain unalienable Rights, that among these are Life, Liberty, and the Pursuit of Happiness—That to secure these Rights, Governments are instituted among Men, deriving their just Powers from the Consent of the Governed, that whenever any Form of Government becomes destructive of these Ends, it is the Right of the People to alter

come destructive of these ends, it is the right of the people to alter or to abolish it, & to institute new government, laying it's foundation on such principles & organizing it's powers in such form, as to them shall seem most likely to effect their safety & happiness. prudence indeed will dictate that governments long established should not be changed for light & transient causes: and accordingly all experience hath shewn that mankind are more disposed to suffer while evils are sufferable, than to right themselves by abolishing the forms to which they are accustomed. but when a long train of abuses & usurpations, begun at a distinguished period, & pursuing invariably the same object, evinces a design to ~~subject~~ reduce them to arbitrary power, it is their right, it is their duty, to throw off such government & to provide new guards for their future security. such has been the patient sufferance of these colonies; & such is now the necessity which constrains them to expunge their former systems of government. the history of his present majesty is a history of unremitting injuries and usurpations, among which no one fact stands single or solitary to contradict the uniform tenor of the rest, all of which

or to abolish it, and to institute new Government, laying its Foundation on such Principles, and organizing its Powers in such Form, as to them shall seem most likely to effect their Safety and Happiness. Prudence, indeed, will dictate that Governments long established should not be changed for light and transient Causes; and accordingly all Experience hath shewn, that Mankind are more disposed to suffer, while Evils are sufferable, than to right themselves by abolishing the Forms to which they are accustomed. But when a long Train of Abuses and Usurpations, pursuing invariably the same Object, evinces a Design to reduce them under absolute Despotism, it is their Right, it is their Duty, to throw off such Government, and to provide new Guards for their future Security. Such has been the patient Sufferance of these Colonies; and such is now the Necessity which constrains them to alter their former Systems of Government. The History of the present King of Great-Britain is a History of repeated Injuries and Usurpations, all having in direct Object the Establishment of an absolute Tyranny over these States. To prove this, let Facts be submitted to a candid World.

have in direct object the establishment of an absolute tyranny over these states. to prove this, let facts be submitted to a candid world, for the truth of which we pledge a faith yet unsullied by falsehood.

He has refused his assent to laws the most wholesome and necessary for the public good.

he has forbidden his governors to pass laws of immediate & pressing importance, unless suspended in their operation till his assent should be obtained; and when so suspended, he has neglected utterly to attend to them.

he has refused to pass other laws for the accommodation of large districts of people unless those people would relinquish the right of representation, in the legislature a right inestimable to them & formidable to tyrants only:

he has dissolved Representative houses repeatedly & continually, for opposing with manly

He has refused his Assent to Laws, the most wholesome and necessary for the public good.

He has forbidden his Governors to pass Laws of immediate and pressing Importance, unless suspended in their Operation till his Assent should be obtained; and when so suspended, he has utterly neglected to attend to them.

He has refused to pass other Laws for the Accommodation of large Districts of People, unless those People would relinquish the Right of Representation in the Legislature, a Right inestimable to them, and formidable to Tyrants only.

He has called together Legislative Bodies at Places unusual, uncomfortable, and distant from the Depository of their public Records, for the sole Purpose of fatiguing them into Compliance with his Measures.

He has dissolved Representative Houses repeatedly, for opposing with manly Firmness his firmness his invasions on the rights of the people:

~~he has dissolved,~~ he has refused for a long space of time to cause others to be elected, whereby the legislative powers, incapable of annihilation, have returned to the people at large for their exercise, the state remaining in the meantime exposed to all the dangers of invasion from without, & convulsions within:

he has endeavored to prevent the population of these states; for that purpose obstructing the laws for naturalization of foreigners; refusing to pass others to encourage their migrations hither; & raising the conditions of new appropriations of lands:

he has suffered the administration of justice totally to cease in some of these colonies, refusing his assent to laws for establishing judiciary powers:

he has made our judges dependent on his will alone, for the tenure of their offices, and amount of their salaries:

he has erected a multitude of new offices by a self-assumed power, & sent hither swarms of officers to harrass our people & eat out their substance:

Invasions on the Rights of the People.

He has refused for a long Time, after such Dissolutions, to cause others to be elected; whereby the Legislative Powers, incapable of Annihilation, have returned to the People at large for their exercise; the State remaining in the mean time exposed to all the Dangers of Invasion from without, and Convulsions within.

He has endeavoured to prevent the Population of these States; for that Purpose obstructing the Laws for Naturalization of Foreigners; refusing to pass others to encourage their Migrations hither, and raising the Conditions of new Appropriations of Lands.

He has obstructed the Administration of Justice, by refusing his Assent to Laws for establishing Judiciary Powers.

He has made Judges dependent on his Will alone, for the Tenure of their Offices, and the Amount and Payment of their Salaries.

He has erected a Multitude of new Offices, and sent hither Swarms of Officers to harrass our People, and eat out their Substance.

he has kept among us in times of peace standing armies & ships of war:

He has kept among us, in Times of Peace, Standing Armies, without the consent of our Legislatures.

he has affected to render the military, independent of & superior to the civil power.

He has affected to render the Military independent of and superior to the Civil Power.

he has combined with others to subject us to a jurisdiction foreign to our constitutions and unacknoleged by our laws; giving his assent to their pretended acts of legislation, for quartering large bodies of armed troops among us:

He has combined with others to subject us to a Jurisdiction foreign to our Constitution, and unacknowledged by our Laws; giving his Assent to their Acts of pretended Legislation:

For quartering large Bodies of Armed Troops among us:

for protecting them by a mock-trial from punishment for any murders which they should commit on the inhabitants of these states;

For protecting them, by a mock Trial, from Punishment for any Murders which they should commit on the Inhabitants of these States:

for cutting off our trade with all parts of the world;

For cutting off our Trade with all Parts of the World:

for imposing taxes on us without our consent;

For imposing Taxes on us without our Consent:

for depriving us of the benefits of trial by jury;

For depriving us, in many Cases, of the Benefits of Trial by Jury:

for transporting us beyond seas to be tried for pretended offenses;

For transporting us beyond Seas to be tried for pretended Offenses:

For abolishing the free System of English Laws in a neighboring Province, establishing therein an arbitrary Government, and enlarging its Boundaries, so as to render it at once an Example and fit Instrument for introducing the same absolute Rule into these Colonies:

for taking away our charters, & altering fundamentally the forms of our governments;

For taking away our Charters, abolishing our most valuable Laws, and altering fundamentally the Forms of our Governments:

for suspending our own legislatures & declaring themselves invested with power to legislate for us in all cases whatsoever:

For suspending our own Legislatures. and declaring themselves invested with Power to legislate for us in all Cases whatsoever.

he has abdicated government here, withdrawing his governors, & declaring us out of his allegiance & protection:

He has abdicated Government here, by declaring us out of his Protection and Waging War against us.

he has plundered our seas, ravaged our coasts, burnt our towns & destroyed the lives of our people:

He has plundered our Seas, ravaged our Coasts, burnt our Towns, and destroyed the Lives of our People.

he is at this time transporting large armies of foreign mercenaries to compleat the works of death, desolation & tyranny, already begun with circumstances of cruelty & perfidy unworthy the head of a civilized nation:

He is, at this Time, transporting large Armies of foreign Mercenaries to compleat the Works of Death, Desolation, and Tyranny, already begun with circumstances of Cruelty and Perfidy, scarcely paralleled in the most barbarous Ages, and totally unworthy of the Head of a civilized Nation.

He has constrained our fellow Citizens taken Captive on the high Seas to bear Arms he has endeavored to bring on the inhabitants of our frontiers the merciless Indian savages, whose known rule of warfare is an undistinguished destruction of all ages, sexes, & conditions of existence:

he has incited treasonable insur- rections of our fellow citizens, with the allurements of for- feiture & confiscation of our property:

he has waged cruel war against human nature itself, violating it's most sacred rights of life & liberty in the persons of a distant people who never of- fended him, captivating & car- rying them into slavery in another hemisphere, or to in- cur miserable death in their transportation thither. this pi- ratical warfare, the oppro- brium of *infidel* powers, is the warfare of the *Christian* king of Great Britain. (~~deter-~~ ~~mined to keep open a market~~ ~~where MEN should be bought~~ ~~and sold,~~) he has prostituted his negative for suppressing every legislative attempt to prohibit or to restrain this

against their Country, to be- come the Executioners of their Friends and Brethren, or to fall themselves by their Hands.

He has excited domestic In- surrections amongst us, and has endeavoured to bring on the Inhabitants of our Frontiers, the merciless Indian Savages, whose known Rule of Warfare, is an undistinguished Destruction, of all Ages, Sexes and Condition.

The Declaration of Independence displayed in the National Archives Building in Washington, D.C.

The Assembly Room in Independence Hall as it has been restored and refurnished to its 1776 appearance

John Trumbull's painting of the signing of the Declaration of Independence

Thomas Jefferson as he was portrayed by John Trumbull in his painting of the signing of the Declaration of Independence

Resolved

That these United Colonies are, and of right ought to be, free and independent States, that they are absolved from all allegiance to the British Crown; and that all political connection between them and the State of Great Britain is, and ought to be, totally dissolved.

That it is expedient forthwith to take the most effectual measures for forming foreign alliances.

That a plan of confederation be prepared and transmitted to the respective Colonies for their consideration and approbation.

The manuscript of Richard Henry Lee's resolution for independence that was submitted to Congress on June 7, 1776

Congress voting independence. Engraved by Edward Savage after Robert Edgepine and Edward Savage.

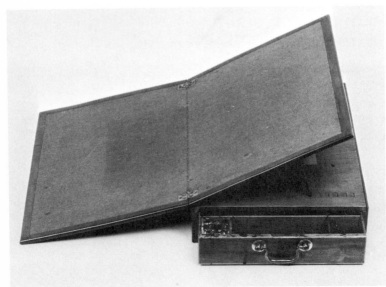

The portable writing desk on which Thomas Jefferson drafted the Declaration of Independence

The first page of Jefferson's rough draft of the Declaration of Independence

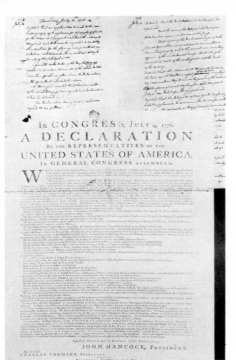

A copy of the Declaration of Independence as printed by John Dunpal on the night of July 4, 1776, which is wafered into the *Journal of Congress*

The title page of the first edition of Thomas Paine's *Common Sense*

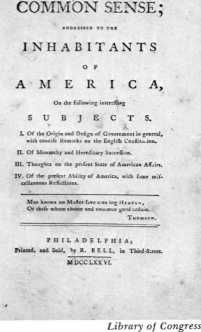

Left: The original engrossed copy of the Declaration of Independence. *Right:* An exact duplicate of the original engrossed copy of the Declaration of Independence with the signatures restored.

Pulling down the statue of George III at Bowling Green, New York City. Engraved by John McRae after Johannes A. Oertel

determining to keep open a market where MEN should be bought & sold:
execrable commerce∧: and
that this assemblage of hor-
rors might want no fact of
distinguished die, he is now
exciting those very people to
rise in arms among us, and to
purchase that liberty of which
he had deprived them, by
murdering the people upon
whom *he* also obtruded them;
thus paying off former crimes
committed against the *liberties* of one people, with crimes
which he urges them to commit against the *lives* of another.

in every stage of these oppressions we have petitioned for redress in the most humble terms;
our repeated petitions have been
answered by repeated injury. a
prince whose character is thus
marked by every act which may
define a tyrant, is unfit to be the
ruler of a people who mean to
be free. future ages will scarce
believe that the hardiness of one
man, adventured within the
short compass of twelve years
only, on so many acts of tyranny without a mask, over a
people fostered & fixed in principles of liberty.

In every stage of these Oppressions we have Petitioned for
Redress in the most humble
Terms: Our repeated Petitions
have been answered only by repeated Injury. A Prince, whose
Character is thus marked by
every act which may define a
Tyrant, is unfit to be the Ruler
of a free People.

Nor have we been wanting in
attentions to our British brethren. we have warned them from
time to time of attempts by their
legislature to extend a jurisdic-

Nor have we been wanting in
Attentions to our British Brethren. We have warned them from
Time to Time of Attempts by
their Legislature to extend an

tion over these our states. we have reminded them of the circumstances of our migration & settlement here, no one of which could warrant so strange a pretension: that these were effected at the expence of our own blood & treasure, unassisted by the wealth or the strength of Great Britain: that in constituting indeed our several forms of government, we had adopted one common king, thereby laying a foundation for perpetual league & amity with them: but that submission to their parliament was no part of our constitution, nor ever in idea, if history may be credited: and we appealed to their native justice & magnanimity, as well as to the ties of our common kindred to disavow these usurpations which were likely to interrupt our correspondence & connections. they too have been deaf to the voice of justice & of consanguinity, & when occasions have been given them, by the regular course of their laws, of removing from their councils the disturbers of our harmony, they have by their free election re-established them in power. at this very time too they are permitting their chief magistrate to send over not only soldiers of our common blood, but Scotch & foreign mercenaries to invade & deluge us in

unwarrantable Jurisdiction over us. We have reminded them of the circumstances of our Emigration and Settlement here. We have appealed to their native Justice and Magnanimity, and we have conjured them by the Ties of our common Kindred to disavow these Usurpations, which, would inevitably interrupt our Connections and Correspondence. They too have been deaf to the Voice of Justice and of Consanguinity. We must, therefore, acquiesce in the Necessity, which denounces our Separation, and hold them, as we hold the rest of Mankind, Enemies in War, in Peace, Friends.

blood. these facts have given the last stab to agonizing affection, and manly spirit ·bids us to renounce forever these unfeeling brethren. we must endeavor to forget our former love for them, and to hold them as we hold the rest of mankind, enemies in war, in peace friends. we might have been a free & great people together; but a communication of grandeur & of freedom it seems is below their dignity. be it so, since they will have it: the road to ~~glory &~~ happiness ^ & to glory^ is open to us too; we will climb it ^apart from them,^ ~~in a separate state~~. and acquiesce in the necessity which ~~pro~~nounces ^de^ our ~~everlasting Adieu!~~ eternal separation!

We therefore the representatives of the United States of America in General Congress assembled do, in the name & by authority of the good people of these states, reject and renounce all allegiance & subjection to the kings of Great Britain & all others who may hereafter claim ·by, through, or under them; we utterly dissolve and break off all political connection which may have heretofore subsisted between us & the people or Parliament of Great Britain; and finally we do assert and declare these colonies to be free and

We, therefore, the Representatives of the UNITED STATES OF AMERICA, in General Congress, Assembled, appealing to the Supreme Judge of the World for the Rectitude of our Intentions, do, in the Name, and by Authority of the· good People of these Colonies, solemnly Publish and Declare, That these United Colonies are, and of Right ought to be, Free and Independent States; that they are absolved from all Allegiance to the British Crown, and that all political Connection between them and the State of independent states, and that as free & independent states they shall have full power to levy war, conclude peace, contract alliances, establish commerce, & to do all other acts and things which independent states may of right do. And for the support of this declaration we mutually pledge to each other our lives, our fortunes, & our sacred honour.

Great Britain, is and ought to be totally dissolved; and that as FREE AND INDEPENDENT STATES, they have full Power to levy War, conclude peace, contract Alliances, establish Commerce, and to do all other Acts and Things which INDEPENDENT STATES may of right do. And for the support of this Declaration, with a firm Reliance on the Protection of Divine Providence, we mutually pledge to each other our Lives, our Fortunes, and our sacred Honor.

Signed by ORDER and IN BEHALF *of the* CONGRESS,
JOHN HANCOCK,
President.
Attest.
Charles Thomson, Secretary.
Philadelphia: Printed by John Dunlap.

With the help of the copy made by Adams, and that made by Jefferson for Lee, on July 8, it is possible to reconstruct the development of the Declaration, from the time that Jefferson first submitted it to Franklin to the time that the committee presented it to the Congress. It may be assumed that the Lee copy is identical with the "fair copy" that Jefferson made for the committee and Congress.

The progression seems to have gone something like this. Jefferson submitted the rough draft—at that point a clean copy, except for eight minor corrections in wording—to Franklin. The old doctor made one, or possibly two, minor verbal changes and passed it to Adams, who made one of his two changes and then made his copy. Jefferson must then have taken the rough draft back and, at a later date, again submitted it to Franklin and Adams, for the next form in which we see it, as evidenced by the Lee copy, shows three more changes of wording in Franklin's hand, one more in Adams', sixteen in Jefferson's, and three added paragraphs, which expand the list of charges against the King. The first of these paragraphs has to do with the "calling together of legislative bodies in places unusual"; the second deals with the enlargement of the boundaries of Quebec; the third with the impressment of seamen into the British navy. Although Jefferson's "Notes" say that the changes of Franklin and Adams were "two or three only, and merely verbal," it is probable that Adams suggested the addition of at least the first of these three paragraphs, because the incident on which it is based occurred in Massachusetts. The paragraph concerning the impressment of seamen also would have come more logically from Adams than from Jefferson, since this was an evil that was of far more concern to Massachusetts and seafaring New England than to the agricultural southern colonies.

Jefferson now made the fair copy that he submitted to the committee. His statement that they reported it "unaltered to the Congress," is reasonable, since the three members who had already agreed on it represented a majority of the committee. Also, Livingston was opposed to the document in any form and Sherman was no writer.

The verbal changes made in the progress of the document through the committee—or through Adams and Franklin— were all undeniably improvements, regardless of who made them. (It is possible that some of those in Jefferson's hand were suggested by his colleagues.) A comparison of the most significant changes in the preamble and the second paragraph indicate this. In the original rough draft the preamble read: "for a people to advance from that subordination in which they have hitherto remained, and to assume among the powers of the earth the equal and independent station . . . etc." The Lee copy reads: "for one people to dissolve the political bands which have connected them with another and assume among the powers of the earth a separate and equal station . . . etc." In terms of flowing prose, this is an obvious improvement.

The most effective changes in the second paragraph include the alteration of "We hold these truths to be sacred and undeniable" to "We hold these truths to be self-evident . . ." Experts are not sure whether this change is in the hand of Franklin or Jefferson, but believe that it was made by the former. Franklin also changed from "reduce them to arbitrary power" to "reduce them under absolute despotism." In the phrase "all men are created equal and independent" the last two words were dropped. ". . . from that equal creation they derive rights inherent and inalienable," was changed to ". . . They are endowed by their creator with equal rights some of which are inherent and inalienable." Congress further altered this to ". . . they are endowed by their creator with inherent and inalienable rights,"—and as has been said, the "inalienable" ultimately became "unalienable," either by mistake or design. A great improvement in style was made by dropping a single word. The phrase "life, liberty, and the pursuit of happiness"

Add P ℼ℔

originally read, "life and liberty and the pursuit of happiness."

Congress made numerous word changes most of which all critics agree were beneficial. Their changes shortened the document by about one-quarter and resulted, in most cases, in better phrasing and the elimination of nonessential words. Of the words remaining in the Declaration, approximately ninety percent are Jefferson's (or the committee's) and ten percent are Congress'. A comparison of the last two sentences in the second paragraph, which contain changes made before and after submission to Congress, indicate the nature of such improvements. Jefferson wrote: "the history of his present majesty is a history of unremitting injuries and usurpations, among which no one fact stands single or solitary to contradict the uniform tenor of the rest, all of which have in direct object the establishment of an absolute tyranny over these states. to prove this, let facts be submitted to a candid world, for the truth of which we pledge a faith yet unsullied by falsehood."

This was finally changed to: "The History of the present King of Great-Britain is a History of repeated Injuries and Usurpations, all having indirect Object the Establishment of an absolute Tyranny over these States. To prove this, let Facts be submitted to a candid World."

Other than verbal changes, the major corrections of Congress were three in number. They eliminated the reference to Scotch mercenaries and softened the criticism of the English people as distinct from the King and government in the next-to-the-last paragraph; they removed entirely the reference to slavery; and they considerably revised the final paragraph. Jefferson was not happy about these changes. In his "Notes" he wrote; "The pusillanimous idea that we had friends in England worth keeping terms with still haunted the minds of many. For this reason those passages which conveyed censures on the people of England were struck out, lest they should give them offense. The clause, too, reprobating the enslaving the inhabitants of Africa was struck out, in complaisance [to] South Carolina and Georgia, who never attempted to restrain the importation of slaves, and who on the contrary still wished to continue it. Our Northern brethren also I believe felt a little tender under those censures; for though their people have very few slaves themselves yet they had been pretty considerable carriers of them to others."

Even after the Declaration had started to become a sacred and immortal document, Jefferson thought that it was better in the form that he had written it than the form in which it was finally proclaimed. In 1818 he wrote, "When the Declaration of Independence was under the consideration of Congress, there were two or three unlucky expressions in it which gave offense to some members. The words 'Scotch and other foreign auxiliaries' excited the ire of a gentleman or two of that country. Severe strictures on the conduct of the British King, in negativing our repeated repeals of the law which permitted the importation of slaves, were disapproved by some Southern gentlemen, whose reflections were not yet matured to the full abhorrence of that traffic. Although the offensive expressions were immediately yielded, these gentlemen continued their depredations on other parts of the instrument."

The elimination of the reference to Scotch mercenaries was surely a wise one—there were many Scots and peoples of Scotch descent in America and there was no point in offending them by indicating that the soldiers of their country were barbarians. A reference to foreign mercenaries was left elsewhere in the document, but this could be construed as applying to the Hessians. From the same paragraph Congress also removed the condemnation of the British people who, Jefferson had written, "have by their free election reestablished . . . in power" the "disturbers of our harmony." At the same time, Congress eliminated the direct reference to the British Parliament, rightly thinking that the justification of rebellion would be stronger if it were confined to charges against a brutal and tyrannical king. While these changes undoubtedly strengthened the Declaration, they also eliminated some of Jefferson's fine phrases: "We must endeavor to forget our former love for them, . . . We might have been a free and great people together."

Adams considered what he called Jefferson's "vehement philippic against negro slavery" one of the best parts of the Declaration, but it did not really belong in the Declaration and Congress was wise to remove it. True, the British government had imposed obstacles when Virginia sought to stop the slave trade, but to blame the evil practice exclusively on George III was too farfetched to be believable. At home, too, there was opposition to the paragraph. The South Carolinians and Georgians favored continuance of the traffic, as did some of their northern brethren, for the simple reason that they were making money out of it.

From a literary standpoint the elimination of the paragraph was small loss. It was out of character with the rest of the Declaration—the rhetoric was forced and stilted, probably because Jefferson's detestation of slavery made him very much emotionally involved, and he was an intellectual rather than an emotional writer—he wrote with his mind rather than his heart. Everything else in the Declaration was logical or philosophical—this paragraph suddenly digressed to present an emotional appeal that did not quite come off. Also, it went off on a tagent to present historical allusions, which did not belong in the Declaration.

Congress' change in the final paragraph made it much stronger than it was in its original form, principally by using, for the renunciation of allegiance, the very wording of the resolution by which independence had been decreed: "That these United Colonies are, and of a right should be, free and independent states; that they are absolved from all allegiance to the British Crown, and that all political connection between them and the State of Great Britain is and ought to be totally dissolved."

Congress also decided that it would be well to intimate that God was on the side of the colonies and added at the beginning of this paragraph the words: "appealing to the Supreme judge of the World for the rectitude of our intentions"; and, at the end: "with a firm reliance on the protection of divine Providence." In his original draft, Jefferson made no reference to the Diety except to recognize "nature's God" in the preamble. During the progress through the committee, a further reference was added in the phrase, "they are endowed by their Creator with certain inalienable rights." This change is in Jefferson's hand but may have been suggested by one of his colleagues.

The Contents of the Declaration

The Declaration of Independence contains four distinct parts or sections; The Preamble, which sets forth the purpose of the Declaration—to "declare the causes which impel them to the separation"; the second paragraph, which presents a philosophy of government based upon the natural rights of men; the long list of charges against the King, which seeks to prove that George III was a tyrant—a despot who was deliberately denying the colonists of their natural rights; and the last paragraph, which contains the actual Declaration of Independence.

Today, the most memorable words in the Declaration of Independence to all Americans are the opening and closing phrases: "When in the course of human events," and "our lives, our fortunes and our sacred honor," and two phrases from the second paragraph; "all men are created equal," and "life, liberty and the pursuit of happiness." The best known and most highly regarded sections of the document are the preamble and the second paragraph. Generations of school-children have been required to memorize the preamble, but it is unlikely that any but a highly specialized student of the subject could even enumerate the charges against the King.

To the members of the Congress that issued this document the emphasis was entirely reversed. Their particular con-cern was for the last paragraph, which contained the Decla-ration of which they had appointed the committee to prepare an announcement. Next in interest were the charges against the King, for here lay their justification for rebel-lion. To the members of Congress the preamble and the following paragraph—the very sections that have made the document immortal—were probably considered as more or less in the nature of window dressing. What was said in them was interesting, necessary, and, perhaps, true; but it was not likely that the kings of France and Spain, brought up under the concept of Divine Right, would be much im-pressed by the idea that governments derived their just powers from the consent of the governed, or by the state-ment that all men are created equal—particularly coming from a society that permitted human slavery. The important part of the second paragraph, to them, was not the political philosophy that it expressed, but the reference to the patient sufferance of the colonies to a long train of abuses and usurpations. These were the facts to be submitted to a can-did world, to prove that the colonies were not rebelling against monarchy, as such, but against tyranny and des-potism.

The Declaration is interesting for what it omits as well as

what it includes. Although virtually all of the preliminary dispute with the mother country had to do with acts of Parliament to which the colonists objected, the Declaration makes no direct reference to the British legislature; the word "Parliament" does not appear in the document, Jefferson's one use of it having been removed—undoubtedly with deliberation—by the Congress. For years the colonists had been screaming against Parliament. The major controversy had centered around the limits of Parliament's authority over the colonies. First the cry had been that Parliament had no right to impose internal taxation; then the claim was made that there could be no "taxation without representation," and finally it had become, simply, no taxation. But in all of this the quarrel was with Parliament—then the Declaration did not even mention Parliament, an omission that was surely deliberate.

There are two indirect references to the British legislature. In one place it says that the King "has combined with others to subject us to a jurisdiction foreign to our constitution." These "others" are obviously the Parliament. Again, the Declaration mentions warnings to the British people "of attempts by their legislature to extend an unwarrantable jurisdiction over us." But these backhanded references do not weaken a primary premise of the Declaration: that it was unnecessary to mention Parliament because that body never did have any authority over the colonies. The position taken in the Declaration was that the only relationship between the inhabitants of the New World and the Empire was a willing and voluntary allegiance to the throne, an allegiance that they were now withdrawing, and had the right to withdraw, because the occupant of that throne was a tyrant who was trying to reduce them to absolute slavery. Their natural rights as free men, they claimed, justified the withdrawal of their allegiance.

Another interesting omission in the Declaration is any reference to the rights of the colonists as Englishmen. This was another change of front. Previously, and as recently as the Declaration of Rights propounded by the First Continental Congress, the colonists had based their claims largely on the grounds that they possessed the rights of English subjects, and that these rights were being violated by certain acts of Parliament. Now they were taking the position that they were not English subjects, except to the extent of their voluntary allegiance to the King. This position was necessary because they could not justify their rebellion in terms of the violation of the rights of British subjects alone. In order to convince mankind of the justice of their position, they had to base their case on the broader theory of the natural rights of all men, not the rights of certain subjects under their patricular government. In the view of those to whom the Declaration was principally addressed—the rulers of potential allies in Europe—subjects of a government could not properly assume a "separate and equal station" among the powers of the earth merely because they objected to the laws of the country to which they belonged. Only by stressing the violation of their rights under the "laws of nature and of nature's God" could they hope to present a convincing case for separation.

In effect, the colonists were expressing a new theory of the British Empire that is nowhere specifically stated in the Declaration but is implied throughout. Under this theory the colonies became a part of the Empire through their own free will, to the extent of a compact between them and the King. Their rights as free men were not impaired by this compact. Therefore, when these rights were violated by the King, they might withdraw from the compact. Under this theory the Parliament and the rights of the colonists as British subjects were irrelevant to the issue and should consequently be ignored in arguing the case.

With regard to the relationship of the colonists to the British people, the Declaration as revised by Congress gave the impression that the colonies parted from them more in sorrow than in anger. It said that the Americans had warned them of improper acts of their legislature; had reminded them of the circumstances of colonial migration; had appealed to "their native justice"; had conjured them "by the ties of our common kindred." But the Britons had been "deaf to the voice of justice and consanguinity," and the colonists must, therefore, sadly "acquiesce in the necessity of separation," and hold them "enemies in war; in peace, friends."

Carl Becker, in his definitive analysis of the Declaration, made this exposition of the theory on which the colonists based their case: "We are not subject to Parliament. We are a free people, whose ancestors, in accord with the natural right of all men, emigrated to the wilds of America, and there established at the hazard of their lives and fortunes new societies, with forms of government suitable to their conditions and agreeable to their ideas. We have our own legislatures to govern us, just as our British brethren have their legislature. The British Parliament, which is their legislature, has no authority over us, any more than our legislatures have authority over them. We do not mention the

British Parliament in our Declaration of Independence because we are not declaring independence of an authority to
which we have never been subject. We are declaring ourselves independent of the king, because it is to the king only
that we have ever been subject; and in dissolving our
connection with the king we separate from the British empire, because it is only through the king that we have ever
had any connection with the British empire. This connection we voluntarily entered into by submitting ourselves to
the sovereign head of the empire. Subjects of the king we
have professed ourselves to be, and loyal subjects, in the
sense that as a free people we acknowledged allegiance to
him personally, thereby freely assuming the obligations that
go with allegiance. But this allegiance to the king, while it
obligates us to support the empire in so far as we can in the
manner we find convenient, gives him no right of compulsion over us. If we separate from the empire, it is because
the king has attempted to exert such compulsion, and by
repeated acts of usurpation has exhibited a determination to
subject us to his arbitrary power. In declaring our independence of the king, and thus separating from the British empire, we are not breaking off a complicated set of intimate
relationships, sanctioned by positive law and long established custom; on the contrary, we are only snipping the
thin gold thread of voluntary allegiance to a personal sov-
reign. As a free people we have formerly professed allegiance to the king as the formal head of the empire; as a free
people we now renounce that allegiance; and this renunciation we justify, not in virtue of our rights as British subjects,
but in virtue of those natural rights which we, in company
with all men, are inalienably possessed of."

The twenty-seven charges against the King that comprise
the bulk of the Declaration were not, in themselves, listed as
justification for rebellion. Rather, they were set down to
prove that the King was *deliberately* trying to subjugate the
colonists to a position bordering on slavery; that he was, in
the words of the Declaration, "a prince whose character is
thus marked by every act which may define a tyrant." Only
by proving that the monarch was consciously and purpose-
fully tyrannical could the colonists justify their renunciation of his rule. The King had a right to veto laws, he had
a right to instruct his governors, he had a right to appoint
Crown officers, he had rights in other matters complained
of by the colonies—but not if he did these things solely or
primarily with "a design to reduce them under absolute
despotism"; not if his acts had as their "direct object the
establishment of an absolute tyranny."

Objective historians on both sides of the Atlantic disagree as to the extent to which Jefferson was justified in
blaming all of the ills of the colonies on George III as an
individual. Many claim that some of his charges do not hold
water, historically. True, they were based on things that
had happened, but it does not follow that all of these things
were caused by acts of the King; and surely they were not
all the result of a settled and deliberate policy on the part of
the King that had as its sole and direct object the subjuga-
tion of the colonies. In fact, the original grievances, based
on Acts designed to produce revenue for the mother country, stemmed from a view which was widely held by the
people of England and the heavily taxed mercantile class—
an opinion which held that the colonies should pay some
part of the cost of military operations that benefited the

colonies. Some of the matters in dispute were blamable on
the stupidity or ignorance of English officials for which the
king was responsible only to the extent that he had appointed the officials. And some grievances stemmed from
instances of obstreperousness on the part of certain colonists.
The Boston Tea Party was a piece of delinquency that so
distressed Benjamin Franklin that he offered to pay for the
tea out of his own pocket.

But it must be remembered that Jefferson was not writing
history—he was making it. It would be going too far to say
that he cared not for the truth of his allegations. Rather, he
was entering a defense for a cause and was concerned with
making the best possible defense, not with writing an impartial or unbiased judgment. Professor Moses Coit Tyler,
in his *Literary History of the American Revolution*, justifies
Jefferson's treatment of the King as follows: "If the Declaration of Independence is now to be fairly judged by us, it
must be judged with reference to what it was intended to
be—namely, an impassioned manifesto of one party, and that
the weaker party, in a violent race quarrel, of a party resolved, at last, upon the extremity of revolution, and already
menaced by the inconceivable disaster of being defeated in
the very act of armed rebellion against the mightiest military power on earth. This manifesto, then, is not to be
censured because, being avowedly a statement of its own
side of the quarrel, it does not also contain a moderate and
judicial statement of the opposite side; or because, being
necessarily partisan in method, it is likewise both partisan
and vehement in tone; or because it bristles with accusations
against the enemy so fierce and so unqualified as now to
seem in some respects overdrawn."

Jefferson's most recent biographer, Dumas Malone, puts it this way: "Jefferson was using the language of political controversy, not of dispassionate scholarship. He was writing as an American partisan, making a case at the bar of public opinion. His personalizing of the grievances and concentrating on the King was not wholly warranted. But to his mind and the minds of the Patriots, the issue had become clear and unescapable. British policy was threatening to destroy liberties that were dearer than life, and this policy was centered in the King, both as a symbol and a person." Shortly before Jefferson wrote the Declaration he had received from Franklin a motto that he adopted for his own seal: "Rebellion to tyrants is obedience to God." Jefferson considered George III a tyrant, therefore it was not important whether the Monarch was personally responsible for every one of the twenty-seven charges that Jefferson made against him—if he was not, he might well have been.

Strangely, the strongest support for Jefferson's view of George III, as expressed in the Declaration, comes from several English historians. Whatever his faults, poor George has not received much support in the histories of his own country where, rightly or wrongly, historians have permitted him to be the scapegoat. According to a respectable body of scholarly British opinion, George III came to the throne with the fixed purpose of regaining for the King many powers and prerogatives which, under the British constitution, did not belong to the Crown. Says Sir Erskine May: "The King desired to undertake personally the chief administration of public affairs, to direct the policy of his ministers, and himself to distribute the patronage of the Crown. He was ambitious not only to reign, but to govern."

The King refused to appoint Prime Ministers whom he could not control. Lord North, who was appointed in 1770, and under whose ministry most of the Revolution was fought, was a mere mouthpiece of the King. "Not only did he direct the minister in all important matters of foreign and domestic policy, but he instructed him as to the management of debates in Parliament, suggested what motions should be made or opposed, and how measures should be carried. He reserved for himself all the patronage . . . [which] was steadily used for the creation and maintenance of a party in both houses of Parliament attached to the King himself. . . . George was, in fact, sole minister during the fifteen years which followed; and the shame of the darkest hour of English history lies wholly at his door." If George was not the despot that Jefferson pictured, the best that can be said for him is that he was ignorant of the true situation in the colonies—stubborn, ill-advised, and perhaps a little bit stupid.

In developing his list of charges against the King, Jefferson stressed those that were based on grievances common to several colonies, although a few were of particular importance to only one or two. Massachusetts had the most complaints—or, at least, complained the most. Virginia was second. In Jefferson's charges the economic matters that had precipitated the breach were kept very much in the background—only one of the twenty-seven charges deals with affairs in which money was the direct cause of discord. The first six charges are concerned with the Monarch's interference with internal legislation, in one way or another.

The first charge accuses the King of refusing "his assent to laws, the most wholesome and necessary for the public good." This had to do with the King's veto power or the royal disallowance of colonial legislative acts. As a policy, this could hardly be blamed on George III since, by their charters, all of the colonies, except Rhode Island, Connecticut, and Maryland, had been required to submit their laws to England for approval for years before he came to the throne. It was a perfectly legal practice that had been followed by such diverse rulers as Charles I and Cromwell, and the first Congress had recognized it in their declaration of rights, as had Jefferson in *Summary View*. But the practice had become evil and burdensome under George III, who struck down more laws and a wider variety of laws than his predecessors. Initially most of the laws disallowed were those that were detrimental to British trade, navigation, or profits, or had other economic disadvantages to the mother country. Jefferson doubtless had also in mind Virginia's laws relative to curbing the slave trade, which were disallowed, as were divorce laws, acts designed to curb the transportation of convicts, and others dealing with the issuance of bills of credit by the colonies and the raising of money by lotteries.

In the next charge Jefferson accuses the King of forbidding royal governors "to pass laws of immediate and pressing importance, unless suspended in their operation till his assent should be obtained; and when so suspended, he has utterly neglected to attend to them." The "suspension clause" for certain types of laws had started in 1708, during the reign of Queen Anne, and had initially been applied principally to laws affecting British economic interests. This charge is really a variation of the first charge, in that the King's failure to act under the suspension clause was equivalent to a disallowance or a veto. The neglect that Jefferson mentions was real and a prime cause of annoyance. The most glaring example was evidenced by a letter from the governor of North Carolina in 1774, urging ratification of a law that had been passed twenty years earlier.

The King, said Jefferson, "has refused to pass laws for the accommodation of large districts of people, unless those people would relinquish the right of representation in the legislature." As the population of the colonies spread westward, their assemblies passed laws creating new counties and townships, which frequently contained clauses that such new divisions should be represented in the legislature. Before the rise of the patriot party in the 1760's, England did not object to this; in fact, in cases in New Hampshire and Pennsylvania, the home government insisted on it. After the French and Indian War, it became apparent the frontier counties and settlements were almost invariably radical and their representatives added to the strength of the patriot party in the legislatures. Consequently, laws creating such new political divisions were usually disallowed unless they did not provide for added membership in the legislature. There were instances of such disallowance in New Hampshire, Massachusetts, New York, New Jersey, and Virginia.

The fourth charge, which accuses the King of calling together "legislative bodies at places unusual, uncomfortable, and distant from the depository of their public records, for the sole purpose of fatiguing them into complaisance with his measures," is principally based on an instance in Massachusetts. In 1768 the governor of that colony, as the representative of the Crown, had called the legislature to meet at Harvard College, in Cambridge, four miles from their normal meeting place. This was done because the legislature objected to meeting in Boston while British troops were stationed there. In the past the legislature had at times met in Cambridge when there was a smallpox scare in Boston. After meeting at their new location for four years, the body claimed that this was distant from their records, illegal, and demanded to return to Boston. The governor replied that he would seek to get them permission to return, but not if they demanded it as a right; he claimed that the King had the right to tell them where to meet. George III then became stubborn and a new governor, General Gage, ordered them to meet in Salem until the King signified his pleasure to permit them to meet in Boston.

"He has dissolved Representative Houses repeatedly, for opposing with manly firmness his invasions of the rights of the people." This was a widespread grievance, principally in connection with the circular letter that Boston sent to the other colonies in 1768. For sending this, the Massachusetts General Court was dissolved, and the legislature of Georgia and South Carolina met a like fate for failing to treat the Massachusets letter "with the contempt it deserves." At other times, the House of Burgesses was dissolved in Virginia.

"He has refused for a long time, after such dissolutions, to cause others to be elected; whereby the legislative powers incapable of annihilation, have returned to the people at large for their exercise; the state remaining in the meantime exposed to all the dangers of invasion from without, and convulsions within." In 1774, all but five colonies had to elect their representatives to the First Continental Congress by conventions, because their legislative bodies had been dissolved and no provision made for their replacement. The colonies justified these extraconstitutional conventions, on the grounds that no legal government existed and that the legislative powers, therefore, returned directly to the people.

With the seventh charge, Jefferson turned from legislation to immigration and land. "He has endeavoured to prevent the population of these states; for that purpose obstructing the laws for naturalization of foreigners; refusing to pass others to encourage their migrations hither, and raising the conditions of new appropriations of lands." Naturalization laws were among those of whose disallowance the colonies complained. In general, they wanted to encourage a certain type of immigrant; the British government felt that such encouragement would be injurious to industrial or agricultural interest at home, because it would rob the mother country of many valuable farmers and artisans. In 1771 a North Carolina act granting a tax exemption to certain Scotch immigrants was disallowed; earlier, a similar Georgia act, which provided tax exemption and free land, met the same fate. Non-English immigrants came from countries unfriendly to England and could be expected to support the patriot party. Also, a man could not hold land nor own a ship unless he was naturalized, and after 1763 the Crown started to disallow acts dealing with naturalization because it did not want to expand the type of citizen who was inclined to rebellion. In 1773 royal governors were instructed to veto all naturalization acts passed by colonial legislatures.

The initial complaint about land also went back to 1763, when the King had declared that all of the land west of the Alleghanies and north of the Ohio was Crown land, not to be settled by pioneers and further ordered all those who had migrated westward to remove. Virginia was particularly alarmed by the order of 1773, which suspended the issuance of land patents, and subsequent royal instructions that all vacant lands be disposed of at auction, reserving to the Crown an annual quit rent of one halfpenny per acre, as well as mineral rights to gold, silver, and precious stones. The basic reason for making land difficult to acquire was that the frontier citizen was inclined to sympathize with the patriot cause.

The eighth and ninth charges dealt with the judiciary. In the first of these, the King was accused of obstructing "the administration of justice, by refusing his assent to laws for establishing judiciary powers." The principal instance of this went back to 1754, six years before George III came to the throne, when a law of North Carolina establishing courts of justice and regulating their proceedings was disallowed because it was claimed that the erection of courts of justice was a prerogative of the King. This dragged on until, in 1773, the Colony had no superior courts, a situation that remained until after the Revolution started. South Carolina, Pennsylvania, and Virginia also had complaints about laws being disallowed which on several occasions caused the normal administration of justice "totally to cease."

The ninth charge dealt with tenure and salary of judges: "he has made judges dependent on his will alone, for the tenure of their offices, and amount and payment of their salaries." This grievance was experienced in Pennsylvania, New York, New Jersey, North Carolina, South Carolina, and Massachusetts. The tenure of English judges had been during good behavior since 1701, but in 1761 the Crown insisted that the tenure of colonial judges should be at the King's pleasure. The principal complaint over salaries paid by the Crown instead of the colonial government was in Massachusetts. The colonists believed that unbiased justice could not be expected from judges who were dependent on the King's pleasure for their jobs and their pay.

The tenth charge went back to the revision of the Sugar Act in 1764 and the accompanying attempt by the mother country to collect import duties. Jefferson claimed that the King "has erected a multitude of new offices, and sent hither swarms of officers to harass our people, and eat out their substance." Most of this "multitude" were the personnel of four new Admiralty Courts in which customs violations were tried. The colonists, like the later frontiersmen, did not like "revenoors." Also, part of the royal patronage involved jobs in the colonies, to which were appointed many individuals who were unacceptable in every way.

The next two charges have to do with the military. The colonists objected because the King "has kept among us, in times of peace, standing armies, without the consent of our legislatures." It was a principal of British liberty, stated in the Bill of Rights of 1689, that "the raising or keeping of a standing army within the kingdom in time of peace, unless it be with the consent of Parliament, is against the law." The colonists felt that their legislatures should have the same authority in this respect as Parliament had at home. After the termination of the French and Indian War in 1763, some of the British troops were not withdrawn from the colonies, and the Quartering Act of 1765 made the colonies liable for their support. Other troops were added after the Stamp Act riots, in 1765, and again in anticipation of enforcing the

Townshend Acts, in 1769. In none of this was approval sought from the legislatures of the colonies in which the troops were stationed.

"He has affected to render the military independent of and superior to the civil power." This refers to the appointment of General Gage as governor of Massachusetts in 1774, while he was commander-in-chief of the British armed forces in America. It is somewhat ironic that Jefferson, after condemning this practice in the Declaration, withdrew as Governor of Virginia during the Revolution, in favor of a military man, an action which he explained by writing: "From a belief that under the pressure of the invasion, under which we were then laboring, the public would have more confidence in a military chief, and that the military commander, being invested with the civil power also, both might be wielded with more energy, promptitude, and effect for the defense of the state, I resigned the administration at the end of my second year, and General Nelson was appointed to succeed me."

At this point in his condemnation of the King, Jefferson involved Parliament by inference, with the charge: "He has combined with others to subject us to a jurisdiction foreign to our constitution, and unacknowledged by our laws; giving his assent to their acts of pretended legislation." The next nine charges relate to acts of Parliament that the Americans considered unconstitutional. These acts are blamed upon the King in the Declaration, since that document does not recognize that Parliament had any authority over the colonies. In a sense these are the most important charges in the Declaration, since they relate to matters that had been the principal subjects of controversy during the preceding thirteen years.

The first mentioned is an act: "For the quartering of large bodies of troops among us." The Quartering Act of 1765 led to the suspension of the New York assembly because that body refused to supply salt, vinegar, and liquor for His Majesty's troops; these commodities being considered as too expensive luxuries. Initially, the Quartering Act covered the support of troops in barracks, but one of the Intolerable Acts extended quartering to private buildings. The colonists felt so strongly about this that a prohibition against it was later embodied in the Bill of Rights in the Constitution.

Still referring to troops, Jefferson charged the King with "protecting them, by a mock trial, from punishment for any murders which they should commit on the inhabitants of these states." This was based on an act of Parliament providing for a change of venue in cases of "persons questioned for any acts done by them in the execution of the law, or for the suppression of riots or tumults in the province of Massachusetts Bay." In such cases, if it appeared to the governor "that an indifferent [impartial] trial cannot be had within the said province" the governor could direct that the case be tried "in some other of His Majesty's colonies, or in England." Obviously a trial in England would be, in the minds of the colonists, a "mock trial" since no English soldier or official would be convicted for doing his duty in suppressing riots.

"For cutting off our trade with all parts of the world" referred to many long standing navigation acts and other measures for the control of trade, of which there were some fifty starting with the Navigation Act of 1660. Most of them were passed long before the reign of George III, but the more recent acts of 1774 and 1775 more drastically curtailed commerce with the colonies, particularly the Prohibitory Act of December 22, 1775 which forbade all trade with the colonies and treated captured colonial property as the goods of an enemy.

The most serious complaint, in relation to the long term controversy, was the shortest; "For imposing taxes without our consent." This referred principally to the Stamp Act and the Townshend Acts, although it could be broadened, under the new thinking toward taxation, to include many long-standing navigation acts that were also revenue producers.

The charge that the King, with Parliament, deprived the colonists "in many cases, of trial by jury" was based on the extension of the jurisdiction of vice-admiralty courts in connection with British efforts to enforce trade and revenue acts. Trial by jury had never been a practice in admiralty courts and offenses against excise laws and acts of trade were tried without a jury in England. From a practical standpoint the acts involved could not have been enforced in the colonies except through the admiralty courts, as it would have been impossible to find a colonial jury that would bring in a conviction against a smuggler.

"For transporting us beyond the seas to be tried for pretended offenses" related to two acts of Parliament. The first had been passed in the reign of Henry VIII and provided that a person accused of treason without the realm might be brought back to England for trial. In 1769 Parliament reminded the King that this act could be applied to the disturbances in America. The other act was passed in 1774, and provided that offenses against the King's property might be tried in England. Both acts were intended to prevent colonial juries of acquitting such offenders, but there is no record of anybody actually being transported under them during the reign of George III.

The next charge was based on the Quebec Act: "For abolishing the free system of English laws in a neighboring province, establishing therein an arbitrary government, and enlarging its boundaries, so as to render it at once an example and fit instrument for introducing the same absolute rule into these colonies." The extension of the boundaries of Quebec to the Ohio River would curtail migration, but the greatest resentment was probably against the extension of the Roman Catholic religion, established by law for the French Canadians, and the French code of laws to which they had always been accustomed. The "arbitrary government" referred to is based on the lack of representative or self-government in Canada and trial by jury.

"For taking away our charters, abolishing our most valuable laws, and altering fundamentally the forms of our government," refers principally to the Massachusetts Government Act of 1774, passed as part of the punishment for the Boston Tea Party. The act changed the mode of selecting juries and the tenure and appointment of the council. These changes, and the provisions for paying the governor's and judges' salary by the Crown, were said to be violations of the colony's charter, which the colonists regarded as fundamental law.

"For suspending our legislatures and declaring themselves invested with power to legislate for us in all cases whatsoever," combines two charges in one. The first is based on the suspension of the New York legislature in the quarrel over the quartering act. The latter part of the sentence obviously refers to the Declaratory Act, which was a part of the repeal of the Stamp Act, under which Parliament asserted its right to legislate for the colonies "in all cases whatsoever."

The remaining five charges are related to the war that had been in progress for over a year. They make the point that George III, by making war on the colonies with all that such action implied, had abdicated his government over the colonies and broken his side of the contract, and the colonists were therefore at liberty to declare the contract null and void. The English considered these the most absurd of the charges in that they sought to use the efforts of the mother country in suppressing a rebellion as justifications for the rebellion.

In the first of these charges Jefferson said: "He has abdicated government here, by declaring us out of his protection and waging war against us." The reference here is to the King's proclamation of August, 1775, in which he declared that a state of rebellion existed, and his warlike speech to Parliament three months later. Originally, Jefferson had included in this charge the phrase "withdrawing his governors." Congress had eliminated this, probably on the grounds that it was too farfetched. The royal governors who had left, had done so a few jumps ahead of a mob or of Continental troops. One, Benjamin Franklin's son William, had been "withdrawn" from the governor's mansion in New Jersey to a jail in Connecticut.

"He has plundered our seas, ravaged our coasts, burnt our towns; and destroyed the lives of our people." This referred to routine acts of war, in which the towns of Falmouth,

Norfolk, Charles Town, and Charleston had been burned or partially burned by the British. Jefferson took the position that the natural consequences of warfare proved the King a despot because that war was being waged by a ruler against his own people.

The charge that: "he is at this time transporting large armies of foreign mercenaries to compleat the works of death, desolation & tyranny, already begun with circumstances of cruelty & perfidy, scarcely paralleled in the most barbarous ages, and totally unworthy the head of a civilized nation" was one of the most effective with the people at home, who seemed to feel that the hired German troops, which had not yet arrived in America, would be a bunch of barbarians who would rape women, wantonly kill children, etc. Such fears were entirely unjustified. Actually, George III was following a long-established English practice in hiring mercenaries. They had previously been used in suppressing rebellions in Scotland and Ireland, and in defeating the French in America.

"He has constrained our fellow Citizens taken Captive on the high Seas to bear Arms against their Country, to become the Executioners of their Friends and Brethren, or to fall themselves by their Hands." This referred to an act passed by Parliament in December, 1775, which authorized capture of vessels and cargoes trading with America "as if the same were ships and effects of open enemies" and further provided that the crews of such vessels might be impressed into the British navy. This reprehensible practice of a navy starved for seamen was not blamable on George III and did not end until after the war of 1812.

The final charge: "He has excited domestic Insurrections

amongst us, and has endeavoured to bring on the Inhabitants of our Frontiers, the merciless Indian savages, whose known Rule of Warfare, is an undistinguished destruction, of all Ages, Sexes and Condition." was based on a threat by Governor Dunmore of Virginia, in 1775, to free slaves who took up arms against the rebels, and on the use of Indian allies by the British. Nothing came of Lord Dunmore's threat and, at the time, the British had not yet made much use of Indians, although they later incited Indian attacks. It is somewhat ironic that at the time Jefferson was writing this, Washington and John Adams favored employing Indians on the American side and a Congressional committee later reported favorably on using them as auxiliaries.

The character of the king was capsulized in the paragraph that followed the charges; "In every stage of these Oppressions we have Petitioned for redress in the most humble Terms: Our repeated Petitions have been answered only by repeated injury. A Prince, whose Character is thus marked by every act which may define a Tyrant, is unfit to be the Ruler of a free People." Two petitions had been sent to the King, by Congress, and he had paid no attention to either of them. Obviously, he did not consider them "humble" petitions, since they asserted that the Parliament had no jurisdiction over the colonies and asked the King to uphold them in this assertion.

The accusation of tyranny on the part of George III in the last part of this paragraph is the substance of Jefferson's justification. This is one of the aspects of the Declaration that was most criticized in England, where it was claimed that none of the charges indicated absolute tyranny or despotism in any commonly accepted sense of the words. It was pointed out that—even if Jefferson's charges were accepted—the King had done nothing in which he had "exceeded the just powers of the Crown as limited by the English Constitution," and that he had never "departed from known established laws and substituted his own will as the rule of his action." As previously stated, there is some difference of opinion on this, but the consensus is that the allegation was stronger than the facts justified. This view was supported by John Adams, who later wrote:

"There were other expressions which I would not have inserted if I had drawn it up—particularly that which called the King a tyrant. I thought this too personal; for I never believed George to be a tyrant in disposition and nature. I always believed him to be deceived by his courtiers on both sides of the Atlantic, and, in his official capacity only, cruel. I thought the expression too passionate and too much like scolding, for so grave and solemn a document; but, as Franklin and Sherman were to inspect it afterwards, I thought it would not become me to strike it out. I consented to report it."

The next-to-last paragraph in the Declaration refers to the colonies' "attentions to our British brethren." These "attentions" were in the form of two addressed to the people of Great Britain, which the Congress adopted in October, 1774, and August, 1775. Other than the "philippic" on slavery that was eliminated altogether, this paragraph received more editing in Congress than any other part of the Declaration. It was here that Jefferson had originally accused the English people of permitting the King "to send over not only soldiers of our common blood, but Scotch & foreign mercenaries to invade & deluge us in blood." In his original draft Jefferson also elaborated his theory concerning the "circumstances of our migration & settlement here," by claiming that, when the colonies were established, "in constituting indeed our several forms of government, we had adopted one common king, thereby laying a foundation for perpetual league & amity with them: but that submission to their parliament was no part of our constitution, nor ever in idea. . . ."

Jefferson's contention was that the colonies represented new societies that had an inherent right to legislative powers and self-government, but which had by their own agreement and consent adopted British law and a recognition of a common sovereign. The common English view was that the powers of the provincial governments were grants from the Crown, rather than that the powers of the Crown were grants from the people of the provinces. The colonial charters, in this view, were not compacts or treaties with autonomous states but acts of domestic legislation. Congress eliminated Jefferson's reasoning on this point from the Declaration, probably because they considered it redundant. The point had already been made, and well made, that the colonists considered themselves tied to the empire only by a voluntary allegiance to the King. A modern scholar has said that Jefferson's theory rested on "a patent misconception of historical facts," but that it was so in tune with the times in the colonies that "nothing else would have served the purpose so well."

The essence of the last paragraph in the Declaration is the actual declaration of independence, inserted by Congress in the exact wording of the resolution to that effect, which had been offered by Richard Henry Lee and adopted on July 2.

The document states that this was done "in the Name, and by Authority of the good People of these Colonies"; and appeals for the approval of "the Supreme Judge of the World." After announcing their independence, the paragraph declares that the colonies are now "FREE AND IN-DEPENDENT STATES," and claims all the powers of sovereign states under international law; "they have full Power to levy War, conclude peace, contract Alliances, establish Commerce, and to do all other Acts and Things which INDEPENDENT STATES may of right do." Here was a simple announcement of the prime purpose for which the Declaration was made—to permit alliances with foreign powers and, in return for their help, to establish commerce with them.

The moving final phrase: "our Lives, our Fortunes, our sacred Honor" was, in more prosaic terms, an expression of the willingness of the colonists to submit to the hardships of taxation and military service.

The contents of the better known first two paragraphs of the Declaration have been analyzed by scholars in several disciplines almost word by word down through the years. In simple terms these paragraphs represent a philosophical justification for rebellion against a tyrannical government; and the following charges against the King sought to prove that his was a tyrannical government. In his *Puritanism and Democracy*, Harvard Professor Ralph Barton Perry expressed it thusly: "The Declaration of Indpendence . . . was a philosophical creed designed to justify the action of men who had taken the law into their own hands. It is at one and the same time a justification of rebellion and a statement of those common principles on which was to be founded a new state. It is as though men should say: 'this is what government and law are for. Judged by this standard, the existing authority has forfeited its claim to obedience. This is at the same time the ground on which to erect a new authority which shall in the future be obeyed as commending itself to our reason and conscience.' "

In the preamble and the first part of the second paragraph Jefferson claimed for the colonists that to which the "laws of nature and of Nature's God" entitled them, and identified these laws with certain "self-evident truths"—that men are "created equal" and endowed by their Creator with certain "unalienable rights," including "life, liberty, and the pursuit of happiness." It is for the achievement of these things, said Jefferson, that "governments are instituted among men."

Many erudite tomes have been written about the meaning of "laws of nature and nature's God." They have been called "fundamental laws," "ancient laws," "the laws of reason," "the laws of God," "the rights of man," "natural rights." Professor Perry gives this definition as the one that Jefferson probably had in mind. "Rational or natural law is neither a mere description of matters of fact, nor a mere definition of the ideal. It is both: it is the law of what ought to be in a world in which things are, normally, what they ought to be. The term 'natural,' as used here, is honorific as opposed to that more modern sense of the term, in which it connotes what is base and rudimentary. Natural law is primitive only in the sense of being prior to civil and religious institutions. It is metaphysical, as affirming the essence of man; moral, as defining the right and the good; rational, in the double sense of being apprehended by reason and applied to rational beings."

Dumas Malone makes the point that this part of the Declaration was better understood when it was written than it is today, in that the terms used, which may seem archaic now, were familiar then to men to whom the theory of natural rights was a fresh and powerful idea. Wrote Malone: "Jefferson saw no need to define terms that the enlightened minds of his time understood, and we can get at the heart of the matter if we regard the word 'rights' as merely the plural of the word 'right' and think of it in the moral sense. Rights, as the people in all ages understand them, are simply what is right. Force does not make right and right derives from no king. Jefferson and his contemporaries found it in the universal law of nature; it arose from the nature of things. It came from God, and what God has given no man can take away; this was inalienable. 'Rights,' therefore, belong to all men because they are men and these rights last as long as life does. . . . Liberty is right and God intends that all men shall have it, and by the same token the force that tyrants use can never be anything but wrong."

Government by "the consent of the governed" substituted a social compact theory for that of divine right, on which monarchy, through the centuries, had been based. Under the social compact theory, all men, in a state of nature, are free, living under nature's laws. A group of individuals may make a compact, may agree or consent to giving up part of their natural liberty to establish a collective government better to protect their most valuable natural rights, defined by Jefferson as "life, liberty, and the pursuit of happiness." In this, Jefferson attacked the theory of absolute monarchy as a form of government that did not involve a social compact with the people—and then sought to prove that George III had constituted himself an absolute monarch by his many acts against the natural rights of the colonists.

The most extraordinary aspect of the Declaration is the compactness and simplicity with which Jefferson expressed the philosophy that, in a few brief sentences, became the foundation of American democracy. But these sentences contain more than simply an expression of a political philosophy. They set forth the reasons that justify the authority of the state: "governments are instituted among men" to secure their "unalienable rights," and their form should be that which "shall seem most likely to effect their safety and happiness." They define the fundamental rights that underlie positive law: men are "created equal," they are entitled to "life, liberty, and the pursuit of happiness"—the aggregate happiness of all individuals is the supreme end of government.

In the second paragraph Jefferson admits that "governments long established should not be changed for light and transient causes," and that, in most cases, "mankind are more disposed to suffer, while evils are sufferable, than to right themselves by abolishing the forms to which they are accustomed." But, he added, the evils to which the colonies had been submitted were no longer sufferable; they represented "a long train of abuses and usurpations, pursuing invariably the same object . . . to reduce them under absolute despotism." In this situation, he averred, "it is their right, it is their duty, to throw off such government, and to provide new guards for their future security." To prove that such a situation existed, he proposed to "let facts be submitted to a candid world . . ."

Jefferson himself explained the meaning and objective of

this part of the Declaration by writing; "With respect to our rights, and the acts of the British government contravening those rights, there was but one opinion on this side of the water. All American Whigs thought alike on these subjects. When forced, therefore, to resort to arms for redress, an appeal to the tribunal of the world was deemed proper for our justification. This was the object of the Declaration of Independence. Not to find out new principles, or new arguments, never before thought of, not merely to say things which had never been said before; but to place before mankind the common sense of the subject, in terms so plain and firm as to command their assent, and to justify ourselves in the independent stand we are compelled to take."

5

The Sources of the Declaration

Perhaps no writer in history has been more widely accused of plagiarism than has Thomas Jefferson for his composition of the Declaration of Independence. Starting shortly after it was released and continuing well into the next century, critics of many hues have accused the Virginian of cribbing ideas and expressions from a multitude of sources.

Jefferson's colleague, Richard Henry Lee, sneered at the document as a thing "copied from Locke's treatise on government." Stephen Carpenter, a Federalist pamphleteer, wrote in the year of Jefferson's retirement from the Presidency that credit for the composition of the Declaration "has been perhaps more generally, than truly, given by the public" to that great man. John Stockton Little described the Declaration as "that enduring monument at once to patriotism and genius, and skill in the art of appropriation." He claimed that, "for the sentiments and much of the language," Jefferson was indebted to Chief Justice Grayson's charge to the Grand Jury of Charleston and to a declaration of independence said to have been adopted by some citizens of Mecklenburg County, North Carolina, in 1775. A Virginia historian, Charles Campbell, traced some of its contents back to a play titled, "The Widow Ranter, or the History of Bacon in Virginia." Even an editor of Jefferson's writings, Paul Leicester Ford, states that a glance at the Virginia Declaration of Rights, adopted in June, 1776, "would seem to indicate the source from which Jefferson derived a most important and popular part" of his Declaration.

The most fervid charge of plagiarism was made by John Adams, in 1822, when he wrote, of the Declaration: "There is not an idea in it, but what had been hackneyed in Congress for two years before. The substance of it is contained in the Declaration of Rights and the violation of those rights, in the *Journal of Congress*, in 1774. Indeed, the essence of it is contained in a pamphlet, voted and printed by the Town of Boston, before the first Congress met, composed by James Otis, as I suppose—in one of his lucid intervals, and pruned and polished by Sam Adams."

The following year Thomas Pickering, a staunch Federalist, quoted Adams' letter in a Fourth of July Address, "to show how little was his [Jefferson's] merit in compiling" the Declaration. This brought from Jefferson a letter to Madison, in which he said: "Pickering's observations, and Mr. Adams' in addition, that it contained no new ideas, that it is a commonplace compilation, its sentiments hackneyed in Congress for two years before, and its essence contained in Otis' pamphlet, may all be true. Of that I am not to be the judge. Rich. H. Lee charged it as copied from Locke's treatise on government. Otis' pamphlet I never saw, and whether I had gathered my ideas from reading or reflection I do not know. I know only that I turned to neither book nor pamphlet while writing it. I did not consider it as any part of my charge to invent new ideas altogether."

The final sentence in the above letter points up the absurdity of the charges of plagiarism of ideas. Jefferson's document would have been worthless had he tried to advance some unique or novel philosophy or system of government. His colleagues in Congress might have agreed with him—or they might not. The people of the colonies might have agreed with him—or they might not. The point is that such was neither his assignment nor was it the object of the Declaration. He had to express ideas that were generally acceptable to the liberals of the day—ideas which, as Adams charged, had been "hackneyed in Congress for two years before."

George Washington defined the background, against which the Declaration was written, in a letter to the governors of the states in 1783: "The foundation of our empire was not laid in the gloomy age of ignorance and superstition; but at an epoch when the rights of mankind were better understood and more clearly defined, than at any former period. The researches of the human mind after social happiness have been carried to a great extent; the treasures of knowledge, acquired by the labors of philosophers, sages, and legislators, through a long succession of years, are laid open for our use, and their collected wisdom may be happily applied in the establishment of our forms of government."

The great merit of Jefferson's creation is that he expressed the liberal ideas that were then in the minds of many men more forcefully and more clearly than they had ever been expressed before. The ideas in the opening part of the Declaration had their place as theories going back to ancient philosophers. Jefferson made them real and cogent and readily comprehensible, and presented them as specific objectives that could be achieved by the society for which he was writing. He expressed his purpose thusly:

"Neither aiming at originality of principle or sentiment, nor yet copied from any particular and previous writing, it was intended to be an expression of the American mind, and to give to that expression the proper tone and spirit called for by the occasion. All its authority rests then on the harmonizing sentiments of the day, whether expressed in conversation, in letters, printed essays, or in the elementary books of public right, as Aristotle, Cicero, Locke, Sidney, etc."

Although Jefferson said that he "turned to neither book nor pamphlet," in writing the Declaration, it seems obvious that he at least had before him some of his own previous writing, or had a remarkable memory. Shortly before he sat down to write the Declaration, Jefferson had submitted some ideas to the Virginia convention that was drawing a constitution for his home colony, which was adopted in June, 1776, as a preamble to that document. This contained twenty charges against George III, which closely paralleled those in the Declaration, and, in some cases, are expressed in identical, or almost identical, verbiage. The charges in the Virginia preamble purport to prove that George III, "intrusted with the exercises of the kingly office in this government, hath endeavored to pervert the same into a detestable and insupportable monarchy," by doing certain things. The first charge read: "By putting his negative on laws the most wholesome and necessary for the public good." In the Declaration this became, as the first charge, "He has refused his assent to laws, the most wholesome and necessary for the public good." The second charge in the Virginia document included the phrase "to pass laws of immediate and pressing importance, unless suspended in their operation for his assent should be obtained." The wording in the Declaration is identical except that "for his assent" becomes "till his assent should be obtained." Eight of the charges are virtually identical in both documents—those relating to standing armies in peacetime, quartering troops, superiority of the military power, cutting off trade, imposing taxes, trial by jury, transporting accused persons to England, and plundering, ravaging and burning.

Of course, borrowing from his own writing could hardly be called plagiarism, but it seems evident, from its rhythm and phrasing, that Jefferson's preamble to the Virginia Constitution was patterned upon part of the English Bill of Rights of 1689, in which was enumerated reasons to justify the overthrow of James II by the English people. In both documents each charge started with the word "by": "By assuming," "By committing," "By refusing," etc., and some of the charges in both documents were similar in sense if not identical in expression.

The most common charge of plagiarism, at the time, related to another section of the Virginia Constitution that had been written by George Mason and incorporated in that document as the Virginia Bill of Rights. The theory of the social compact, of government based on the rights of man, which is the basis of the opening of the Declaration, is also the basis of Mason's Bill of Rights, which starts with the statement: "That all men are by nature equally free and independent, and have certain inherent rights, of which, when they enter into a state of society, they cannot, by any compact, deprive or divest their posterity; namely, the enjoyment of life and liberty, with the means of acquiring and possessing property, and pursuing and obtaining happiness and safety." Jefferson said the same thing in the words: "all men are created equal, that they are endowed by their Creator with certain unalienable rights, that among these are life, liberty, and the pursuit of happiness."

Mason said: "That all power is vested in, and consequently derived from, the people; that magistrates are their trustees and servants, and at all times amenable to them. That government is, or ought to be, instituted for the common benefit, protection, and security, of the people, nation, or community"; Jefferson said: "That to secure these rights, governments are instituted among men, deriving their just powers from the consent of the governed."

On the subject of the right of rebellion, Mason said: "Whenever any government shall be found inadequate or contrary to these purposes, a majority of the community hath an indubitable, unalienable, and indefeasible right, to reform, alter, or abolish it, in such manner as shall be judged most conducive to the publick weal." Jefferson expressed the same idea by writing: "whenever any form of government shall become destructive of these ends, it is the right of the people to alter or to abolish it, and to institute new government, laying its foundation on such principles, and organizing its powers in such form, as to them shall seem most likely to effect their safety and happiness."

There is obviously a similarity of ideas here and, since the Virginia Constitution was adopted on June 12, 1776, and reached Congress while Jefferson was writing the Declaration, it was perhaps natural to assume that the earlier document was the basis of the latter one. But such an assumption is not necessarily valid. The ideas were no more original with Mason than they were with Jefferson. They were part of the Enlightenment. Not only had they been expressed by many Americans, in one form or another, during the years when trouble with England was brewing, but they had formed the basis of much of the writing of French, German, and English philosophers and political theorists for more than a century.

The earliest view of Jefferson's basic source was that he had leaned on Jean Jacques Rousseau, particularly the Frenchman's *Social Contract*. This seems unlikely because latter research has revealed that there is no clear evidence that Jefferson had read Rousseau. Further, *Social Contract* was not published until 1762, and the essential ingredients of the ideas expressed in the Declaration were abroad in the colonies before that time, albeit they had but a limited following.

The more prevalent theory is that Jefferson's inspiration was the English philosopher, John Locke, particularly his *Second Treatise of Government*, of which it has been said that "the principles of the American revolution were in large part an acknowledged adoption of the ideas it contained." When Locke wrote his *Two Treatises of Government*, in 1690, he was, like Jefferson, seeking to justify a rebellion; in Locke's case the English revolution of 1688. Jefferson's Declaration was animated by "a decent respect for the opinions of mankind." Locke's *Treatises* were, in his words, written: "to establish the throne of our great restorer, our present King William; to make good his title, in the consent of the people . . . and to justify to the world the people of England, whose love of their just and natural rights, with their resolution to preserve them, saved the nation when it was on the very brink of slavery and ruin."

The *Second Treatise of Government* begins with the state of nature from which all commonwealths spring—a state of nature that is social in character and in which men are subject to the law of reason which teaches that no one ought to harm another in his life, health, liberty, or possessions. There is, however, in this state of nature, no common superior to enforce the law of reason; each individual must work out his own interpretation. The result is confusion and inconvenience and the possibility that peace among men may be so precarious as to verge on anarchy. To remedy this, government is instituted through the medium of a contract, a social compact, under which each individual agrees with every other to give up to the community the right of enforcing the law of reason, in order that life, liberty, and property may be preserved. The compact with the government is not general, but limited and specific; the natural right of enforcing the law or reason alone is given up; the natural rights reserved to the individual limit the power of the community or government.

Government, established by the consent of the people, becomes the supreme power in the community, but it is not arbitrary. It is in the nature of a trust and embraces only such powers as were transferred to it by the change from a state of nature. It must exercise its power through standing laws and authorized judges; no man can be deprived of his property without his consent, nor can taxes be levied without the consent of the people or their representatives. Finally, the legislature cannot transfer its powers to any other person or body—its power is delegated by the people, who alone can alter it. As is evident, Locke's maxims were the basis of the United States Constitution, and they applied to the British government when he wrote them in 1690. Later, with the rise of the British Empire, Parliament became omnipotent and, by 1776, had, in effect, transferred its powers to the King, by whose patronage it was controlled.

It was a cardinal point of Locke's theory that the power of the people was superior to that of the government and that under certain conditions government could be dissolved. He wrote: "There remains still in the people a supreme power to remove or alter the Legislative, when they find the Legislative act contrary to the Trust reposed in them." The people had the right of rebellion, but, he added, only when government had become unfaithful to its trust, and revolution should not be the act of a minority. Locke did not specify the grounds nor the manner in which the people were justified in repossessing themselves of the government power, but he did make the point that between the government and the people there can be no judge except the people themselves—that public opinion was the ultimate judge.

Scholars have gone through Locke's *Second Treatise* with a fine-tooth comb to find the exact paragraphs from which

Jefferson got the ideas and expressions contained in the second paragraph of the Declaration. In connection with the phrase, "all men are created equal," they quote Locke to the effect: "Men, being, as has been said, by nature all free, equal, and independent, no one can be put out of this estate and subjected to the political power of another without his own consent. . . . When any number of men have so consented to make one community or government, they . . . make one body politic, wherein the majority have a right to act and conclude the rest." It is obvious, however, that Jefferson had absorbed this concept of the equality of men long before he wrote the Declaration. It was inherent in the pronouncement of Roman jurists, whom Jefferson had studied, that all men were equal under law. As a youth, he had copied a similar sentiment from the Greek poet, Euripides, in his literary commonplace book, a statement that translates to: "Nature gave men the law of equal rights." He had read John Milton's justification of the execution of Charles I, in which he said, "No man who knows aught, can be so stupid to deny that all men are born free." Finally, Jefferson had used this premise in one of his early law cases in which he argued, in 1770, that statutes that imposed servitude on the child of a mulatto could not operate upon a grandchild; also, since, "Under the law of nature, all men are born free."

Locke wrote extensively on the law of nature, specifically: "The state of Nature has a law of Nature to govern it, which obliges every one, and reason, which is that law, teaches all mankind who will but consult it, that being all equal and independent, no one ought to harm another in his life, health, liberty, or possessions."

The law of nature was at once reasonable and divine—
Thomas Aquinas said that natural law was the participation
of rational beings in the eternal law. In his theories Locke
stressed reason over revelation. In his *Second Treatise* he
referred to the law of nature as the command of God but
the theological reference was not of primary importance, as
it had been in the medieval Christian thinking that preceded
the Age of Enlightenment. Locke gave to the law of nature
a specific political meaning that was set forth in terms of
"natural rights," which, although they had a priority in
natural law, might be limited by agreement among individuals who willingly placed themselves under authority of
government. But political sanction does ont supersede the
divine and natural law that is "unwritten, and so nowhere
to be found but in the minds of men." Locke expounds this
thought by writing: "The obligations of the law of Nature
cease not in society, but only in many cases are drawn
closer, and have, by human laws, known penalties annexed
to them to enforce their observation. Thus the law of
Nature stands as an eternal rule to all men, legislators as
well as others. The rules that they make for other men's
actions must . . . be conformable to the law of Nature; i.e.,
to the will of God, of which that is a declaration, and the
fundamental law of Nature being the preservation of mankind, no human sanction can be good or valid against it."

Although Jefferson's expression, "the laws of nature and
of nature's God," finds a basis in Locke, it was part of the
"rights of man" theory that had wide acceptance during the
Enlightenment and to say that Jefferson specifically took it
from Locke is unwarranted. Scholars have tried to trace his

very wording to other writers, with whom Jefferson was familiar, and have quoted from Pope's *Essay on Man:*

> Slave to no sect, who takes no private road,
> But looks through Nature up to Nature's God.

Also, there appears in Jefferson's commonplace book a passage that he quoted, in his youth, from Bolingbroke: "One follows Nature and Nature's God; that is, he follows God in his works and in his word."

Perhaps the phrase in the Declaration that has been subjected to more scholarly "nit-picking" than any other, is: "life, liberty, and the pursuit of happiness." Locke wrote of "life, liberty, and fortunes," "life, liberty, and estate," "life, health, liberty, and possessions," and said that "government has no other end but the preservation of property." He defined property as that which a person has removed "out of a state that Nature hath provided and left it in" and "hath mixed his labor with it"; he added: "The supreme power cannot take from any man part of his property without his own consent."

Locke expressed the theory that the primary purpose for which government was organized and accepted by man was for the protection of his property, thusly: "If a man in the state of Nature be so free as has been said, if he be absolute lord of his own person and possessions, equal to the greatest and subject to nobody, why will he part with his freedom, this empire, and subject himself to the dominion and control of any other power? To which it is obvious to answer, that though in the state of Nature he hath such a right, yet the enjoyment of it is very uncertain and constantly exposed to the invasion of others; for all being kings as much as he, every man his equal, and the greater part no strict observers of equity and justice, the enjoyment of the property he has in this state is very unsafe, very insecure."

"Life, Liberty, and property" was a rather common phrase in colonial documents before Jefferson wrote the Declaration. The resolutions adopted by the First Continental Congress, in 1774, had declared that the colonists were entitled to "life, liberty, and property." A few months previously the Boston Committee of Correspondence had stated: "We are entitled to life, liberty, and the means of sustenance." A year earlier the Massachusetts Council had asserted: "Life, liberty, property, and the disposal of that property, with our consent, are natural rights." George Mason, in the Virginia Bill of Rights, had mentioned both property and happiness as among the natural rights of men, inferentially distinguishing between them, "the enjoyment of life and liberty, with the means of acquiring and possessing property, and pursuing and obtaining happiness and safety."

Some have argued that Jefferson's failure to accept the popular form of the phrase indicated that he did not believe in or approve of private property, that he leaned toward some form of socialism—an opinion that is patently absurd to anyone who is familiar with all of Jefferson's writings. Ray Forrest Harvey, biographer of Jean Jacques Burlamaqui, reasoned that the difference between Locke's statements and Jefferson's indicated that their theories were opposed. He argues that Burlamaqui was responsible for "pursuit of happiness" and quotes from the Swiss philosopher's *Principles of Natural Law*, published in 1747, to this effect: "My design is to inquire into those rules which nature alone prescribes to man, in order to conduct him safely to the end, which every one has, and indeed ought to have, in view; namely, true and solid happiness. By *happiness* we are to understand the internal satisfaction of the soul, arising from the possession of good; and by good, whatever is suitable or agreeable to man for his preservation, perfection, conveniency, or pleasure. The idea of good determines that of evil, which in its most general signification, implies whatever is opposite to the preservation, perfection, conveniency, or pleasure of man. . . . Right . . . is nothing else but whatever reason certainly acknowledges as a sure and concise means of attaining happiness, and approves as such."

At a much later date, James Wilson of Pennsylvania had written, in 1774, that the happiness of the governed was the prime purpose of government: "All men are, by nature, equal and free; no one has a right to any authority over another without his consent; all lawful government is founded on the consent of those who are subject to it; such consent was given with a view to ensure and to increase the happiness of the governed, above what they could enjoy in an independent and unconnected state of nature. The consequence is, that the happiness of the society is the *first* law of every government."

Jefferson was familiar with the writings of Burlamaqui—he had copied excerpts from him in his commonplace book. And he surely knew Wilson's pamphlet from which the above quotation is taken. But it does not follow that the "pursuit of happiness" phrase is based on either. As a phrase it had been used by Dr. Samuel Johnson and in other eighteenth-century works of literature. Nor does his change from "property" to "happiness" indicate any divergence between his theory and Locke's. Jefferson undoubtedly did not list property as an inalienable natural right because he considered it as a means to happiness, not an end in itself. In any event the undisturbed possession of property was certainly embraced in the pursuit of happiness, in Jefferson's thinking, just as property, or estate, or possessions were but ingredients of happiness in Locke's.

The English political philosopher had often acknowledged his debt to Richard Hooker, who wrote a century earlier than Locke. As a link between medieval thinking and the Enlightenment, Hooker was more concerned with the Divine aspects of natural law, but he recognized that natural law took cognizance of human desires and the material things necessary for their satisfaction when he wrote: "All men desire to lead in this world a happy life. That life is led most happily, wherein all virtue is exercised without impediment or let. The Apostle, in exhorting men to contentment, although they have in this world no more than very bare food and raiment, giveth us thereby to understand that those are even the lowest of things necessary; that if we should be stripped of all those things without which we might possibly be, yet these must be left; that destitution in these is such an impediment, as till it be removed suffereth not the mind of man to admit any other care. . . . Inasmuch as righteous life presupposeth life; inasmuch as to live virtuously it is impossible except we live; therefore the first impediment, which naturally we endeavour to remove, is penury and want of things without which we cannot live. Unto life many implements are necessary; more, if we seek (as all men naturally do) such a life as hath in it joy, comfort, delight, and pleasure."

Unquestionably, Jefferson's phrase, substituting happiness for property, was a more inclusive and far-reaching expression of the philosophy than any that had been previously used. Happiness put the matter on a moral plane; property did not. The English scholar, John Morley, in his study of Edmund Burke, described the profound effect of this phrase by writing: "Much ridicule, a little of it not altogether undeserved, has been thrown upon the opening clause of the Declaration of Independence, which asserts the inherent natural right of man to enjoy life and liberty, with the means of acquiring and possessing property, and pursuing and obtaining happiness and safety. Yet there is an implied corollary in this which enjoins the highest morality that in our present state we are able to think of as possible. If happiness is the right of our neighbor, then not to hinder him but to help him in its pursuit, must plainly be our duty. If all men have a claim, then each man is under an obligation. The corollary thus involved is the cornerstone of morality. It was an act of good augury thus to inscribe happiness as entering at once into the right of all, and into the duty of all, in the very head and front of the new charter, as the base of a national existence, and the first principle of a national government. . . . The assertion in the New World, that men have a right to happiness and an obligation to promote the happiness of one another, struck a spark in the Old World."

Jefferson's concept of the social compact theory of government, as opposed to the divine-right theory of absolute monarchy, which he expressed in the words: "Governments

are instituted among men, deriving their just powers from
the consent of the governed" may be found in Locke, and
many other places. This, too, was part of the thinking of
the Enlightenment. In a passage already quoted, Locke said:
"Men being, as has been said, by nature all free, equal, and
independent, no one can be put out of his estate and subjected to the political power of another without his own
consent." In another passage, Locke, citing Hooker, declares that the legislative power cannot be exercised except
by "the hands where the community have once placed it . . .;
for without this, the law could not have that which is absolutely necessary to its being a law, the consent of the society,
over whom nobody can have a power to make laws but by
their own consent and by authority received from them."
Elsewhere he writes: "the governments of the world, that
were begun in peace, had their beginning laid on that foundation, and were made by the consent of the people."

By the time that Jefferson wrote the Declaration, the idea
that God spoke only through kings and that they, therefore,
had a Divine right to rule, had been questioned for more
than two centuries. The phrase, "*Vox populi, vox Dei*," had
long been in use. The *just* rights of kings, like any other
form of government, derived from the people, as John
Milton said in *The Tenure of Kings and Magistrates*; "[It
is] manifest that the power of Kings and Magistrates is nothing else, but what is only derivative, transferred and omitted
to them in trust from the people, to the common good of
them all, in whom the power yet remains fundamentally,
and cannot be taken from them, without a violation of their
natural birthright."

The "consent of the governed" theory had been expressed

in previous colonial writings. In 1773 the Massachusetts House quoted Locke and Hooker when it said, in answer to a speech by Governor Hutchinson, "It is consent alone that makes human law binding." John Dickinson had written in 1774 that the "freedom of a people consists in being governed by laws in which no alteration can be made without their consent." In fact, the early battle cry of the colonial rebellion: "taxation without representation" was, in effect, an expression of the injustice of government without the consent of the governed. Jefferson needed to go to no specific source for this fundamental political philosophy.

Jefferson's theory—"whenever any form of government becomes destructive to these ends, it is the right of the people to alter or abolish it"—found justification in Locke, and other sources. Locke said, "There remains still in the people a supreme power to remove or alter the legislature," but only if there had been a breach of trust; he wrote that the public power was to be obeyed, "unless there be reason showed which may necessarily enforce that the law of reason or of God enjoin the contrary." Locke gave five situations in which this would be the case:

"Where the ruler sets up his own arbitrary will in place of the laws; where he hinders the legislative power 'from assembling in its due time or from acting freely'; where he alters the mode of electing the legislative representatives of the people; where he delivers the people into subjection to a foreign power; and where he abandons his trust and fails to put the laws in execution." It will be noted that all but the fourth of these instances of dissolution of government are embodied in charges against George III in the Declaration of Independence; and perhaps the use of Hessian troops might even be regarded as delivering the people into the hands of a foreign power. "These events have," said Locke, "the effect of altering the legislative power"; and "When any one, or more, shall take upon them to make laws whom the people have not appointed to so do, they make laws without authority, which the people are not therefore bound to obey." Locke continues, in language which is echoed in the Declaration, "when the government is dissolved, the people are at liberty to provide for themselves by erecting a new legislative differing from the other by the change of persons, or form, or both, as they shall find it most for their safety and good. . . . Whensoever, therefore, the legislative shall . . . endeavour to grasp themselves, or put into the hands of any other, an absolute power over the lives, liberties, and estates of the people, by this breach of trust they forfeit the power the people had put into their hands for quite contrary ends, and it devolves to the people, who have a right to resume their original liberty, and by the establishment of a new legislative (such as they shall think fit), provide for their own safety and security, which is the end for which they are in society."

Locke limited the right to rebellion, or the right to change the government, to cases where government had violated its trust, or its compact with the people. John Milton, in *The Tenure of Kings and Magistrates*, went further and maintained that the people had the right to change government at will; "since the King or Magistrate holds his authority of the people, both originally and naturally for their good in the first place, and not his own, then may the people as oft as they shall judge it for the best, either choose him or reject him, retain him or depose him, though no Tyrant, merely by the liberty and right of freeborn Men, to be governed as seems to them best."

The right of a people to rebellion—to "alter or abolish" the government by which they had been ruled—was the whole point that Jefferson was trying to prove with the Declaration. In that document his thinking followed Locke rather than Milton; he showed that there was clear evidence of a breach of trust. Subsequently, the United States Constitution followed Milton rather than Locke, in that it provided for a referendum to alter the government at stated intervals.

Jefferson needed no support from Locke or anybody else to adopt the theory of the right of rebellion. He liked the slogan that Franklin gave him—"Rebellion to tyrants is obedience to God"—so much that he incorporated it in his seal. Later, when President George Washington marched at the head of troops to suppress the farmers who had fomented the Whiskey Rebellion, Jefferson wrote: "God forbid we should ever be twenty years without . . . a rebellion. The people cannot be all, and always, well informed. The part which is wrong will be discontented in proportion to the importance of the facts which they misconceive. If they remain quiet under such misconceptions, it is a lethargy, the forerunner of death to the public liberty. . . . What country can preserve it's liberties if their rulers are not warned from time to time that their people preserve the spirit of resistance? Let them take arms. The remedy is to set them right as to facts, pardon and pacify them. . . . The tree of liberty must be refreshed from time to time with the blood of patriots and tyrants. It is it's natural manure."

There are a couple of instances in the Declaration in

which Jefferson's wording is identical with that used by Locke. The phrase "more disposed to suffer" is found in Locke; "the people . . . are more disposed to suffer than right themselves by resistance." Likewise, "a long train of abuses" is an expression used by Locke; "such revolutions happen not upon every little mismanagement in public affairs. . . . But if a long train of abuses, prevarications, and artifices, all tending the same way, make the design visible to the people . . . it is not to be wondered that they should then rouse themselves."

The charge that George III sought to "establish an absolute tyranny over these states" was rejected at the time by many English writers, who sought to prove that the King operated within the law. The difference here was on the definition of the word "tyranny." Jefferson followed Locke here, when the latter said, "tyranny is the exercise of power beyond right."

As a basis for his political ideas, Jefferson did not need to go abroad, for they were in full accord with principles embodied in the earliest American charters, and the American mind had been prepared for their reception for a century and a half. The charter of Maryland, dating back to 1632, provided that Lord Baltimore and his heirs should make laws "consonant with reason" and agreeable to the laws, statutes, customs, and rights of . . . England." There were similar provisions in the Fundamental Orders of Connecticut, issued in 1639; in the Massachusetts Body of Liberties, 1641; and in William Penn's Frame of Government of Pennsylvania, 1682. In the First Continental Congress John Adams was insistent that the colonies should "recur to the law of nature, as well as the British Constitution, and our American charters and grants."

Dumas Malone, in his *Jefferson and His Times,* has this to say about the source of Jefferson's ideas for the Declaration; "Before the imperial crisis became acute in 1774-1775 and he first had occasion to present his political ideas in an important way, the doctrine of natural rights was one of his postulates. Just where he got it is a fascinating question, but one to which it seems impossible to give a specific answer. If he did not draw on John Locke in the first place but got the ideas of that noted writer secondhand, he certainly had his very phraseology by heart in 1776."

Professor Carl Becker, a notable authority on the Declaration of Independence, says, "Where Jefferson got his ideas is hardly so much a question as where he could have got away from them," and has this to say about Locke: "So far as the 'Fathers' were, before 1776, directly influenced by particular writers, the writers were English, and notably Locke. Most Americans had absorbed Locke's works as a kind of political gospel; and the Declaration, in its form, in its phraseology, follows closely certain sentences in Locke's second treatise on government. This is interesting, but it does not tell us why Jefferson, having read Locke's treatise, was so taken with it that he read it again, and still again, so that afterwards its very phrases reappear in his own writing. . . . Generally speaking, men are influenced by books which clarify their own thought, which express their own notions well, or which suggest to them ideas which their minds are already predisposed to accept."

Professor Tyler, in his *Literary History of the American Revolution,* not only justifies but praises Jefferson for his acumen in basing the Declaration on ideas and phrases that had long been in the minds of liberal men on both sides of the Atlantic. When the Act of Independence was passed and the Virginian was selected to draw up its announcement, Professor Tyler asks, "What, then, was Jefferson to do? Was he to regard himself as a mere literary essayist, set to produce before the world a sort of prize dissertation—a calm, analytic, judicial treatise on history and politics with a particular application to Anglo-American affairs—one essential merit of which would be its originality as a contribution to historical and political literature? Was he not, rather, to regard himself as, for the time being, the very mouthpiece and prophet of the people whom he represented, and, as such, required to bring together and to set in order, in their name, not what was new, but what was old; to gather up into his own soul, as much as possible, whatever was then also in their souls—their very thoughts and passions, their ideas of constitutional law, their interpretations of fact, their opiinons as to men and as to events in all that ugly quarrel; their notions of justice, of civic dignity, of human rights; finally, their memories of wrongs which seemed to them intolerable, especially of wrongs inflicted upon them during those twelve years by the hands of insolent and brutal men, in the name of the King, and by his apparent command?

"Moreover, as the nature of the task laid upon him made it necessary that he should thus state, as the reasons for their intended act, those very considerations both as to fact and as to opinion which had actually operated upon their minds, so did it require him to do so, to some extent, in the very language which the people themselves, in their more formal and deliberate utterances, had all along been using. . . . While the Declaration of Independence lacks originality in the sense just indicated, in another and perhaps a higher sense, it possesses originality—it is individualized by the character and the genius of its author. Jefferson gathered up the thoughts and emotions and even the characteristic phrases of the people for whom he wrote, and these he perfectly incorporated with what was already in his own mind; and then to the music of his own keen, rich, passionate, and enkindling style, he mustered them into that stately and triumphant procession wherein, as some of us still think, they will go marching on to the world's end."

6

The Reception of the Declaration

From one end of the country to the other, as fast as it could be spread among the people, the Declaration was greeted with demonstrations of delight. In show-business parlance it might be said that it got rave reviews. Except for a few opinions expressed privately, the public reception was a paean of praise. So far as the Declaration itself was concerned, this opinion was largely nonobjective. It was the *act* of independence, rather than the substance or form of its announcement, that chiefly excited the people. They accepted the Declaration's political philosophy, uncritically, as commonplace. Those who were ready to accept *a* declaration of independence readily accepted *the* Declaration of Independence. From Philadelphia, where the Congress sat, and from every colony, letters carried the opinions of colonial leaders as to the Declaration's meaning and effect.

On July 5, John Adams wrote to a friend of his wife's: "I will inclose to you a Declaration, in which all America is most remarkably united.—It compleats a Revolution, which will make as good a Figure in the History of Nations, as any that has preceded it—provided always that the Ladies take Care to record the Circumstances of it, for by the Experience I have had of the other Sex, they are either too lazy or too active to commemorate it." And to Abigail he added, "There is a most amiable, laudable and gallant Spirit prevailing, in these middle Colonies. The Militia turn out in great Numbers and in high Spirits, in New Jersey, Pennsylvania, Maryland, and Delaware."

William Whipple wrote to John Langdon on July 8: "This Declaration has had a glorious effect—has made these colonies all alive." And, perhaps concerned with Tory reaction, he added, "I hope that you will take care that the Declaration is properly treated." Joseph Barton of Delaware wrote to his cousin, of the Declaration: "It gives a great turn to the minds of our people declaring our independence. Now we know what to depend on. For my part, I have been at a great stand. I could hardly own the King, and fight against him at the same time; but now these matters are cleared up. Heart and Hand shall move together. I don't think there will be five Tories in our part of the country in ten days after matters are well known. We have had great numbers who would do nothing until we were declared a free State, who now are ready to spend their lives and fortunes in defense of our country."

From New Jersey, Jonathan Elmer wrote: "With the independence of the American states a new era in politics has commenced. Every consideration concerning the propriety or impropriety of a separation from Britain is now entirely out of the question. Our future happiness or misery, therefore, as a people depend entirely upon ourselves."

Samuel Adams wrote, in one letter: "It must be allowed by the impartial World that this Declaration has not been made rashly. . . . Much I fear has been lost by Delay, but an Accession of several Colonies has been gained by it." And in another: "Our Declaration of Independency has given Vigor to the Spirits of the people. Had this decisive Measure been taken Nine Months ago, it is my opinion that Canada would at this time have been in our hands. . . . We were more fortunate than I expected in having 12 of the 13 Colonies in favor of the all important Question. The Delegates of N.York were not empowered to give their Voice on either side—their Convention has acceded to the Declaration & Published it even before they received it from Congress— so mighty a Change in so short a Time!"

Samuel Cooper wrote from Boston: "We receiv'd last Saturday by the Post the Declaration. It is admir'd for its Comprehensive & calm Dignity." Also from Massachusetts, Tristram Dalton wrote to Elbridge Gerry: "I wish you joy on the late full Declaration—an event so ardently desired by your good self and the people you particularly represent. We are no longer to be amused with delusive prospects. The die is cast. All is at stake. The way is made plain. No one can now doubt on which side it is his duty to act. . . . We are not to fear what man or a multitude can do. We have put on the harness, and I trust it will not be put off until we see our land a land of security and freedom—the wonder of the other hemisphere—the asylum of all who pant for deliverance from bondage."

From Virginia, John Page wrote to his boyhood friend, Thomas Jefferson: "I am highly pleased with your Declaration. God preserve the United States. We know the Race is not to the swift nor the Battle to the strong. Do you not think an Angel rides in the Whirlwind & directs this Storm?" From Pennsylvania, Benjamin Rush wrote: "The Declaration of Independence has produced a new era in this part of America. The Militia of Pennsylvania seem to be actuated with a spirit more than Roman. . . . The Tories are quiet, but very surly. . . . The spirit of liberty reigns triumphant in Pennsylvania. . . . I think the Declaration of Independence will produce union and new exertions in England in the same ratio that they have done in this country." And again from Rush: "The influence of the declaration of independence upon the senate & the field is inconceivable." In a third letter several months later, the doctor wrote: "The declaration of independence was said to have divided & weakened the colonies. The contrary of this was the case. Nothing but the signing, & recognizing of the declaration of independence preserved the congress from dissolution in Decem 1776, when Howe marched to the Delaware. . . . But, further, the declaration of independence produced a secession of tories—timid—moderate & double-minded men from the counsels of America, in consequence of which the congress as well as each of the states have possessed ten times the vigor and strength they had formerly."

Richard Henry Lee, after comparing the copy that Jefferson had made for him before the document went to Congress with the copy printed by Dunlap, commiserated with his fellow Virginian by writing: "I wish sincerely, as well for the honor of Congress as that of the States, that the manuscript had not been so mangled. It is wonderful, it is passing pitiful, that the rage of change should be so unhappily applied. However, the *Thing* in its nature is so good, that no cookery can spoil the dish for the palates of freemen."

The commendation of the Declaration was widespread but not entirely unanimous. Robert Morris said in reply to a letter from New York: "I am sorry to say there are some amongst us that cannot bear the thought of Reconciliation on any terms . . . I cannot help Condemning this disposition as it must be founded in keen Resentment or in interest Views. . . . I have uniformly voted against & opposed the declaration of Independence because in my poor opinion it was an improper time and will neither promote the interest or rebound to the honor of America, for it has caused division when we wanted Union, and will be ascribed to very different principles than those, which ought to give rise to such an Important measure."

The reception of the Declaration in Canada may be inferred from an item in the *Pennsylvania Gazette*, which read: "The Governor of Halifax received the Declaration of Independency, about four weeks since, but would not permit the poor dupe of a printer (had he ever so good a mind) to publish any more of it than barely the last clause, where it says: 'We, therefore, the Representatives of the United States of America in General Congress assembled, Do &c., &c. And his reason (as we are credibly informed) was 'because it may gain over to them (the rebels) many converts; and inflame the minds of his Majesty's *loyal* and *faithful* subjects of the province of Nova-Scotia.' "

In France the Declaration was received with acclaim by

the people, and with less enthusiasm by the government. De Condorcet wrote that it was not enough that the rights of man, "should be written in the books of philosophers and in the hearts of virtuous men; it is necessary that ignorant or weak men should read them in the example of a great people. America has given us this example. The act which declares its independence is a simple and sublime exposition of those rights so sacred and so long forgotten." Mirabeau said: "The sublime manifesto of the United States of America was very generally applauded." The Marquis de Lafayette conspicuously placed a copy of the Declaration in his house, leaving beside it a vacant place to be filled, he said, by a declaration of rights for France when, if ever, France should have one.

Securing help from France was one prime purpose of the Declaration, but the most important man in this connection, French Foreign Minister the Comte de Vergennes, did not officially receive it for several months. The original letter from Congress to the American commissioner, Silas Deane, went astray. He received a copy on August 17. This letter, wrote Dean, "was very far from relieving me, as it inclosed what had been Circulated thro' Europe for two months before, and my pretending to inform this Court, could be only a matter of form." This does not explain why he did not transmit the Declaration to de Vergennes until November 20, on which date he advised the minister, in part, "I have the honor to deliver to your Excellency, the enclosed Declaration of Independence of the United States of North America, and to inform you that by the first of said Letters, the Congress appears to have been unanimous in this important resolution. . . . They also say . . . the Declaration of

Independence meets with universal Approbation, and the people seem everywhere animated still more by it in defence of their Country."

If the Congress expected that their proclamation of independence would have the immediate effect of securing a French alliance, they were disappointed. That country, in fact, did not formally acknowledge it. De Vergennes told him, Deane wrote Jay, that "unless France, by a public Acknowledgement of your independency, makes war on G. Britain in your favor, what service can such Acknowledgement be of to the United States? You are known here. Our Ports are open, & free for your Commerce, and your Ships are protected in them, and greater indulgencies allowed than to any other Nation. If France should be obliged to make War on England, it will be much more just, and honorable, in the Eyes of the World to make it on some other Account, & if made at all, it is the same thing to the United States of America, &, in one important View, better for them to have it Originate from any other Cause, as America, will be under the less immediate Obligation— further, France has Alliances, and cannot resolved a Question which must, perhaps, involve her in a War, without previously Consulting them; meantime, the United States can receive the same succours & Assistance from France, without as well as with such an open Acknowledgement, perhaps much more advantageously."

In the interests of France, de Vergennes favored a policy of aiding the colonies as much as possible—unofficially; but young Louis XVI of France could not be expected heartily to endorse a document which proclaimed that governments derive their just powers from the consent of the governed.

It was not until word was received in Paris of the American victory at Saratoga in October, 1777, that de Vergennes could successfully propose a formal alliance to Louis. It now seemed evident that the Americans might represent the winning side. Even then, the young King tried to shilly-shally, claiming that he could not sign such a treaty without the approval of his "brother" in Spain. It required a push from the wily Dr. Franklin to bring the issue to a head. After Saratoga, Lord North had sent an agent, Paul Wentworth, to Paris, with an offer of reconciliation. Franklin refused to see him until the King proposed the lengthy delay involved in consulting Spain. Franklin then sent for Wentworth and confused the British agent with an afternoon of double-talk. Wentworth reported to Lord North that he could not understand why the old man, who was known for his directness, seemed to be talking in circles and saying nothing. Franklin had nothing to say to Wentworth—but he knew that the meeting would promptly be reported to de Vergennes, who would fear that reconciliation was in the wind—a most undesirable development from the French standpoint. The foreign minister quickly advised Franklin that the King's council had decided to recognize the independence of the United States. Six weeks later, a treaty of commerce was signed and a separate treaty of alliance that had as its aim "to maintain effectually the liberty, sovereignty, and independence of the United States."

In England the Declaration received mixed notices. The King and the ministry, obviously, condemned it, while some Whigs were surprisingly outspoken in their endorsement. In his speech opening the House of Lords, the King said, "So daring and desparate is the Spirit of those Leaders, whose Object has always been Dominion and Power, that they have now openly renounced all Allegiance to the Crown, and all political Connection with this Country. They have . . . presumed to set up their rebellious Confederacies for Independent States. If their Treason be suffered to take Root, much Mischief must grow from it, to the Safety of my loyal Colonies, to the Commerce of my Kingdoms, and indeed to the present System of all Europe. One great Advantage, however, will be derived from the Object of the Rebels being openly avowed, and clearly understood. We shall have Unanimity at Home, founded in the general Conviction of the Justice and Necessity of our Measures."

George was unduly optimistic about the degree of unanimity. When a proposal was made to endorse the sentiments of his speech, several Lords spoke against it. The Marquis of Rockingham said that, if the colonies had "declared themselves independent, it was long after they were declared enemies; and for his part he could not possibly see what degree of obedience was due, where public protection was openly withdrawn."

The Duke of Richmond thought it would be much better to have the Americans "as friends than enemies, though we should be under the necessity of acknowledging them as so many independent States"; and, in speaking of the various measures that preceded the Declaration, he said that the "Ministers had been successful, and gained what they secretly wished for, though they did not dare to avow it."

The Duke of Grafton "pledged himself to the House, and to the publick, that while he had a leg to stand on, he would come down, day after day, to express the most marked abhorrence of the measures hitherto pursued, and meant to be adhered to, in respect to America. He condemned, in terms equally explicit and unreserved, the measures which had compelled America to declare herself independent, though he was sorry for it, and thought she acted extremely wrong in so doing."

In an address to the King, from the House of Commons, the Declaration was condemned with the words: "we cannot forbear to express our detestation and abhorrence of the audacious and desperate spirit of ambition, which has at last carried those leaders so far, as to make them openly renounce all allegiance."

But here, too, opinion was far from unanimous. Fox thought "The Americans had done no more than the English had done against James II." The Honorable Temple Luttrell said, "For his part, he construed this speech [the King's] an infamous, groundless libel fabricated by a tyrannical faction, against some of the most valuable members of the British community, who, actuated by principles of justice and honour, were nobly contending on the other side of the Atlantick, for the dearest rights of mankind; and who, limiting their resistance to a redress of real and essential grievances, were falsely accused of having, from the beginning of this unhappy contest, had no other object in view than anarchy and indepedence."

John Wilkes said, of the King's ministers, "They drove the Americans into their present state of independency." And Governor Johnstone allowed that "he was far from being pleased with the Americans for their declarations in favour of Independency, but he saw clearly that they were driven to the measure by our vigorous persecution of them."

And at least one English mother was firmly on the side of

the Americans, or so it would seem from this item quoted from an English paper: "Sunday morning last the wife of a journeyman bricklayer in Petticoat Lane, was delivered of three children who were baptised by the names of *Hancock*, *Adams* and *Washington*. Hancock died the day of his birth, but Adams and Washington are in perfect health."

As in Parliament, press reaction was mixed, and dependent on the political views of the journal reporting. The *Scots Magazine* editorialized: "The Declaration is, without doubt, of the most extraordinary nature, both with regard to sentiment and language; and considering that the motive of it is to assign some justifiable reasons of their separating themselves from G. Britain unless it had been fraught with more truth and sense, it might well have been spared, as it reflects no honour upon either their erudition or their honesty."

The *Morning Post*, of August 19, believed that the Declaration would have an effect in Europe opposite to that hoped for by the colonists: "The Congress have acted with the utmost impolicy, in declaring the United Colonies free and independent States; for, after such an avowal of their Republican principles, every European Power must now abandon them to the punishment due to their Villainy and folly."

The Whig *Gazetteer* saw in the Declaration, and the policy of the ministry which led to it, a grave blow to the British Empire: "We have lost America forever; hopes of a reconciliation are fled even from those who have plunged us into these distresses. The secret counsels of a few are the cause of all this mischief; and it become the public of all ranks to turn their eyes and attention to those few, and make them answerable for their conduct. . . . The people cry out to their Sovereign for the lives of their fellow subjects, lost in a fruitless, inglorious, contest. They cry out for justice against those by whose counsels half the British Empire is lost, the treasures of the nation wasted, its forces employed in wreaking the revenge of a few; the safety of the kingdom endangered, and the reputation both of Prince and people tarnished in the eyes of all Europe." And in a later article this same paper predicted that France and Spain would be quick to take advantage of England's discomfiture. "The trade with America we have irrecoverably lost, and our good friends, the French and Spaniards, are at length in quiet possession of that inexhaustible mine of treasure. They now enjoy unmolested what they have a long time secretly endeavored to obtain. . . . The American trade has too many allurements to escape the attention and pursuit of the French and Spanish Courts. They laugh at the idea of our Ministry, in expecting to withhold the intercourse of commerce upon a private dispute between a King and his subjects, as to the last degree absurd. But to carry on that farce, they will amuse us with promises which they have no intention to keep, and feed our Ministry with vain expectations of neutrality."

There were two lengthy and detailed rebuttals of the Declaration printed in pamphlet form and widely circulated in England. One, titled "Strictures upon the Declaration of the Congress at Philadelphia," was written by Thomas Hutchinson, ex-Governor of Massachusetts. The colonists had a particular dislike for Hutchinson because, unlike most other royal governors, he was American-born, yet a more ardent royalist than any of his colleagues. Some letters that he wrote to an unknown peer in England, in 1768-69, were part of the fuel that fed the flames of rebellion. These missives, which advocated stern punitive measures by the Crown against Massachusetts, fell into the hands of Benjamin Franklin in London, who sent them in confidence to the Massachusetts legislature. Someone, probably Samuel Adams, let the damning documents leak to the press, which resulted in a public investigation of Franklin's conduct by a committee of the Parliament and a vicious condemnation of the old man.

"Strictures" started with a lengthy review of events during the twelve years before the outbreak of violence, which Hutchinson described as evidence of a diabolical plot on the part of a few men in each colony to mislead the people and rouse them to open rebellion. The protestations of these men, through the years, that they did not want independence were, said Hutchinson, barefaced lies, put forth because the time was not yet ripe. Independence had always been the aim of these wily villains, who expected great personal gain from the removal of British authority.

Hutchinson criticized the Preamble to the Declaration on these grounds: "They begin with a false hypothesis, That the Colonies are one *distinct people*, and the kingdom another, connected by *political* bands. The colonies, *politically* considered, never were a distinct people from the kingdom. There never has been but one *political* band, and that was just the same before the first Colonists emigrated as it has been ever since; the Supreme Legislative Authority, which hath essential right, and is indisputably bound to keep all parts of the Empire entire."

He ignored the philosophy expressed in the second paragraph entirely, except rhetorically to ask the delegates of the southern colonies how they could call liberty an inalienable right of man while "depriving more than one hundred thousand Africans of their rights to Liberty." He added that he would not attempt "to confuse the absurd notions of government, or to expose the equivocal or inconclusive expressions contained in this Declaration."

The balance of "Strictures" answered each of the charges against the King, individually. In general, Hutchinson's position was that some of the charges had no basis in fact, and that the acts upon which other charges were based were either trivial or merely a continuation of the policies of previous monarchs—policies which the colonists had always heretofore acknowledged as being legal and right. His answer to the charge that the King had caused legislative bodies to meet in places "unusual, uncomfortable, and distant from the depository of their public records, for the sole purpose of fatiguing them" was amusing. He pointed out that the legislative body had previously met in Cambridge, on several occasions of smallpox scares, so the place was not unusual; the meeting hall at Harvard and the quarters for representatives in private homes in Cambridge were far from uncomfortable; and four miles could hardly be called distant. As to fatiguing, he recalled that the body called a meeting for every day, which required the governor to attend; then, as soon as the governor got there, they adjourned. If anybody was fatigued, it was the governor.

The other rebuttal was written by John Lind, under the title, "An Answer to the Declaration of the American Congress." This was better written, better reasoned, and more objective than Hutchinson's. Lind started by claiming that to lay the blame on the King personally, was to confuse and misguide; "the dispute is not, *nor never has it been,* between his *Majesty* and the *whole,* or any *part,* of his subjects. The dispute is *clearly between one part of his subjects and another.* The blow given by the Congress appears indeed to be levelled at his *Majesty;* but the wound was intended for *us.*" Therefore, he said, the Declaration was an insult to every Englishman.

Lind pointed out that the attitude of the colonists through the past few years had been utterly inconsistent. "Their *first attacks* were cautious; the *Ministry* only were to blame: To rail at Ministers, is always popular. The King was deceived; the Parliament misled; the nation deluded." When this was not effective, "Parliament came in for its share of culpability. It encroached on the rights of the American Assemblies. . . . Still, the King was their common Father; the nation, their brethren." Later, "the King ceased to be their father. Still, the nation were their brethren, their friends. . . . At last they perceived that those friends could not serve the turn expected of them, could no more misguide the nation, than deceive the King and Parliament. And now King, and Parliament, and nation, and patriots, and friends, are *all* involved in one common accusation, all pointed out as objects of one common odium."

Like Hutchinson, Lind brushed off the first two paragraphs of the Declaration. The meat of it in his mind, as in most minds of the time, was not the philosophy of government expressed in the opening, but the specific charges against the King. Wrote Lind, "Of the preamble I have taken little or no notice. The truth is, little or none does it deserve. The opinions of the modern Americans on Government, like those of their good ancestors on witchcraft, would be too ridiculous to deserve any notice, if like them, too, contemptible and extravagant as they be, they had not led to the most serious evils."

Most of Lind's "Answer" was a detailed refutation of each charge made against the King, which he treated with cool logic. On that of imposing taxes, for instance, he wrote, "This was originally the *apparent* object of contest. Nor could anything have been found more proper to work upon the people. Such is the selfishness inherent in human nature, that men in general are but too apt to seize any pretence for evading the obligation of paying the servants of the Public. To hold forth such a pretence, must be a sure road to popularity, and to all that power which popularity can give. Like the Agrarian law among the Romans, it is a standard to which the multitude would naturally flock." Lind continued to point out taxation was nothing new in the reign of George III. The colonies had always been taxed by revenue-producing navigation bills. "No new power was, for the first time, assumed."

On the charge involving the change in the government of Quebec, Lind pointed out that this change was actually the repeal of a law enacted at the end of the war that restricted the Catholic religion and the old system of civil laws; and that this repeal had been in response to a petition from the Canadians. In one charge the King was being called a tyrant because he *did not* heed a petition from the thirteen colonies; in another charge he was being called a tyrant because he *did* heed the petition from Canada.

As to other changes in charters, the subject of another charge, Lind pointed out that the charters of several colonies had been changed under previous monarchs by acts that repealed the original charters. There had been changes in the charters of Pennsylvania and Maryland under King William, in those of Connecticut and Rhode Island under Queen Anne, in that of Massachusetts under George I. In fact, Lind observed, "If charters, once granted, could not be altered, could not be repealed, by the Crown, the original Virginia charter would be still in force; the revolted Colonies would be reduced to two; and the inhabitants dependent on two trading companies, *residing in England*."

In response to the charge that the King had made the military independent of and superior to civil power, Lind pointed out that in 1756, before George came to the throne, Lord Loudon had been commander-in-chief of the armies that fought the French, as well as Governor of Virginia, and had been succeeded in both posts by Jeffrey Amherst. The colonies did not complain about this and; "The form of the Commisison, the powers conveyed by it, remain the same to this hour: by his present Majesty, no alteration has been made; no new powers have been conveyed to the Commander-in-Chief." Further, in connection with mercenaries, Lind claimed that foreign troops were used in America against the French and welcomed by the colonists, who then saw nothing barbarous in the practice.

And so, Lind reasonably knocked down charge after charge, proving the King not guilty of tyranny or usurpation of power, principally because "nothing was done but what former Kings and former Parliaments have shewn theirselves ready to do, had the same circumstances subsisted. The same circumstances never did subsist before, because, till the present reign, the Colonies never dared to call in question the supreme authority of Parliament." Lind performed his job so well, that had the King been on trial before an impartial jury, with Jefferson's charges representing the case for the prosecution and Lind's *Answer* the case for the defense, George III would almost certainly have been acquitted.

Summarizing English opinion, William Lee wrote from London, on September 10: "The declaration of independence on the part of America, has totally changed the nature of the contest between that country and Great Britain. It is now on the part of Great Britain a scheme of conquest, which few imagine can succeed. Independence . . . has altered the face of things here. The Tories, and particularly the Scotch, hang their heads and keep a profound silence on the subject; the Whigs do not say much, but rather seem to think the step a wise one, on the part of America, and what was an inevitable consequence of the measures taken by the British Ministry."

The over-all meaning of the Declaration, to Europe, was expressed thus by the early-American historian, George Bancroft: "The civilized world had the deepest interest in the result; for it involved the reform of the British Parliament, the emancipation of Ireland, the disenthralment of the people of France, the awakening of the nations of Europe. Even Hungary stretched forward to hear from the distance the gladsome sound; the Italians recalled their days of unity and might. . . . In Spain, the interest in America was confined to the Court . . . the Catholic King was averse to hostile measures; his chief minister wished not to raise up a republic on the western continent, but only to let England worry and exhaust herself by a long civil war."

7

Opinions on the Declaration

Probably no public paper has ever more perfectly satisfied the immediate purpose for which it was created than did the Declaration of Independence. If it did not immediately bring gold, ships, and men from Europe to support the patriot cause, it surely struck a spark that flamed into later help. And it did much to inspire patriotic effort and unity back home. But, in later years, before it became sacred and immortal, opinion of the merits of the Declaration was far from uniform. Abraham Lincoln said, "The principles of Jefferson are the definitions and maxims of a free society." Rufus Choate referred contemptuously to "the glittering and sounding generalities of natural right which make up the Declaration of Independence." Between these two opinions there lay a range of viewpoints on the document that verged from saintly white to devilish black.

To most modern Americans it might seem that adversely criticizing the Declaration of Independence is of a piece with condemning motherhood—an almost treasonable profanity. But the paper has been criticized, and widely. Said Professor Tyler, late in the nineteenth century, "From the date of its original publication down to the present moment, it has been attacked again and again, either in anger or in contempt, by friends as well as by enemies of the American Revolution, by liberals in politics as well as by conservatives. It has been censured for its substance, it has been censured for its form, for its misstatements of fact, for its fallacies in reasoning, for its audacious novelties and paradoxes, for its total lack of all novelty, for its repetition of old and threadbare statements, even for its downright plagiarisms; finally, for its grandiose and vaporing style."

There is literally no statement in the Declaration that somebody, at some time, has not challenged. Even the inalienability of man's right to life was questioned by Justice Holmes, who, in a case involving the military draft, pointed out that men were being marched off to fight without any regard to a supposed right to life. His ruling said, "The most fundamental of the supposed pre-existing rights—the right to life—is sacrificed without a scruple not only in war but whenever the interest of society—that is, the predominant power in the community—is thought to demand it."

Many have pointed out that the concept of liberty is at variance with the concept of law. The same Justice Holmes observed that "pretty much all law consists in forbidding men to do some things that they want to do." In his rebuttal of the Declaration, John Lind elaborated on this by writing: "The rights of *'life, liberty,* and *the pursuit of happiness'*—

by which, if they mean anything, they must mean the right to *enjoy* life, to *enjoy* liberty, and to *pursue* happiness—they '*hold to be unalienable.*' This they 'hold to be among the *truths self-evident.*' At the same time, to secure these rights, they are content that governments should be instituted. They perceive not, or will not seem to perceive, that nothing that can be called government ever was, or ever could be, in any instance, exercised, but at the expence of one or other of those rights. That, consequently, in as many instances as government is ever exercised, some one or other of these rights, pretended to be unalienable, is actually alienated."

The theory of natural law and the rights of man, which was accepted as commonplace by liberals in the eighteenth century, lost much of its high prestige in the nineteenth century. Many considered the "truths" of Jefferson's Declaration to be "naïve truths"; theoretically obtainable in some Utopia perhaps, but not applicable to practical political affairs. The United States had by this time established "a more perfect union," and its leaders were far more interested in keeping it that way than in change, even if such change were labeled as progress to the high ideals of Jefferson's document. Jefferson's theories were fine as the basis of revolutionary movement, but revolutionary movements were out of fashion now. His ideas were labeled as common sense in the seventeenth century, but, in the words of Carl Becker, "What seems but common sense in one age often seems but nonsense in another."

The most general criticism of the Declaration revolved around the question of slavery. The slave-holding South had never accepted the "free and equal" idea. At the Virginia constitutional convention shortly before the Declaration was written there was much objection to this concept in George Mason's Bill of Rights, where the planter members saw it "as being the forerunner or pretext of civil convulsion." They were mollified by assurances that it was only a figure of speech and, in any event, obviously did not apply to slaves.

The original northern states put the "free and equal" phrase in the preambles to their constitutions: Massachusetts, "all men are born free and equal, and have certain unalienable rights"; New Hampshire, "all men are born equally free and independent." The new western states picked up such expressions, in most cases, when they drafted their constitutions. But the southern states made one tiny change in wording that allowed for their "peculiar institution," within the framework of the concept. Alabama, Arkansas, Florida, Kentucky, Mississippi, and Texas changed the wording to "all freemen, when they form a social compact, are equal."

In the new states that were formed during the first half of the nineteenth century, the adoption of these sentiments in state constitutions may be mainly attributed to the conventional acceptance of a great tradition. During the thirty years before the Civil War, the ideas of Jefferson's second paragraph were generally ridiculed by political leaders, North and South, as fallacies—as "glittering generalities." It was somewhat difficult in the South to depart from the words of the great Virginian; but perhaps Jefferson did not mean what he said. Governor James Henry Hammond of South Carolina explained that "our forefathers, when they proclaimed this truth (that all men were created equal) to be

self-evident, were not in the best mood to become philosophers, however well calculated to approve themselves the
best of patriots. They were much excited, nay, rather angry.
They were angry with George III; and what they meant to
assert was only that kings and nobles and Englishmen were
no better than simple American freemen. If Jefferson meant
more than that, it must be ascribed to the fact that he was
unduly influenced by the French school of thought. The
phrase was simply a finely sounding one, significant of that
sentimental French philosophy, then so current, which was
destined to bear such sanguinary consequences."

Only the abolitionists, a radical minority until the outbreak of the Civil War, waived the Declaration to prove
that there was a "higher law" than the positive law of the
Constitution. Their cause was based not on the legal rights
of American citizens but on the sacred and inalienable rights
of all men, as proclaimed in the Declaration. To answer this
point of view, John C. Calhoun wrote his "Disquisitions on
Government," which presented a new version of "nature's
laws," and the equality of men thereunder. It might well be,
he admitted, that all men are equal in a state of nature,
"meaning, by a state of nature, a state of individuality, supposed to have existed prior to the social and political state,
and in which men lived apart and independent of each
other." In such a state all men would, indeed, be free and
equal. "But such a state is purely hypothetical. It never did,
nor can exist, as it is inconsistent with the preservation and
perpetuation of the race. It is, therefore, a great misnomer to
call it *the state of nature*. Instead of being the natural state
of man, it is, of all conceivable states, the most opposed to
his nature, most repugnant to his feelings, and most incom-

patible with his wants. His natural state is the social and political—the one for which his Creator made him, and the only one in which he can preserve and perfect his race. . . . It follows that men, instead of being born in it (the so-called state of nature), are born in the social and political state; and, of course, instead of being born free and equal, are born subject not only to parental authority but to the laws and institutions of the country where born, and under whose protection they draw their first breath."

If the Declaration of Independence countenanced the wild talk and treasonable acts of the abolitionists, then its self-evident truths must be merely abstractions, unsupportable in a practical world. Rufus Choate asked, "Is it man as he ought to be, or man as he is that we must live with . . . ? Do you assume that all men . . . uniformly obey reason . . . ? Where on earth is such a fool's paradise as that to be found?" The Whigs, he said, must unite against the new Republican party, "it's mission to inaugurate freedom and put down oligarchy, its constitution the glittering and sounding generalities . . . [of] the Declaration of Independence."

Yet, though leaders in government and commerce were willing to set aside the ideals of the Declaration in the interest of maintaining a peaceful and profitable *status quo*, a great segment of the American people were not so casual about the doctrine that had brought their nation into being. Writes Professor Tyler: "The logic of Calhoun was as flawless as usual, when he concluded that the chief obstruction in the way of his system, was the preamble of the Declaration of Independence. Had it not been for the inviolable sacredness given by it to those sweeping aphorisms about the natural rights of man, it may be doubted whether, under the vast practical inducements involved, Calhoun might not have succeeded in winning over an immense majority of the American people to the support of his compact and plausible scheme for making slavery the basis of the republic. It was the preamble of the Declaration of Independence which elected Lincoln."

Abraham Lincoln never had any second thoughts about the verity of the philosophy of the Declaration. Speaking in Independence Hall, on Washington's birthday in 1861, he said, "I have never had a feeling politically that did not spring from the sentiments embodied in the Declaration of Independence. I have often pondered over the dangers which were incurred by the men who assembled here, and framed and adopted the Declaration of Independence. I have pondered over the toils that were endured by the officers and soldiers of the army who achieved that Independence. I have often inquired of myself what great principle or idea it was that kept this Confederacy so long together. It was not the mere matter of the separation of the Colonies from the motherland; but that sentiment in the Declaration of Independence which gave liberty, not alone to the people of this country, but, I hope, to the world, for all future time. It was that which gave promise that in due time the weight would be lifted from the shoulders of all men."

Professor Carl Becker, in his far-reaching analysis of the Declaration of Independence, which he labeled "a study in the history of political ideas," concluded a discussion of the philosophy of the Declaration by writing: "To ask whether the natural-rights philosophy of the Declaration of Independence is true or false is essentially a meaningless question. When honest men are impelled to withdraw their allegiance to the established law or custom of the community, still more when they are persuaded that such law or custom is too iniquitous to be longer tolerated, they seek for some principle more generally valid, some 'law' of higher authority, than the established law or custom of the community. To this higher law or more generally valid principle they then appeal in justification of actions which the community condemns as immoral or criminal. They formulate the law or principle in such a way that it is, or seems to them to be, rationally defensible. To them it is 'true' because it brings their actions into harmony with a rightly ordered universe, and enables them to think of themselves as having chosen the nobler part, as having withdrawn from a corrupt world, in order to serve God or Humanity or a force that makes for the highest good. . . . The natural-rights philosophy of the Declaration of Independence was one formulation of this idea of a higher law. It furnished at once a justification and a profound emotional inspiration for the revolutionary movements of the seventeenth and eighteenth centuries. Founded upon a superficial knowledge of history it was, certainly; and upon a naïve faith in the instinctive virtues of human kind. Yet it was a humane and engaging faith."

Despite the many and varied criticisms of its philosophy, the Declaration became and has remained the foundation on which American Democracy has rested for almost two centuries. Much has changed, but the ideals of the Declaration still have an unshakable hold on the minds of Americans. Professor Ralph Barton Perry put it this way: "The Declaration of Independence contains the essential ideas of American democracy, and has remained its creed and standard throughout the years of its subsequent development. 'For the first time in the history of the world,' says Professor Corwin, 'the principles of revolution are made the basis of settled political institutions.' These principles have been challenged by individual thinkers, and even, as in the epoch of the Civil War, by sections or classes; but they have invariably been invoked in times of crisis or of patriotic fervor as constituting the moral bond of American nationality. . . . They have proved broad enough to embrace partisan differences and cycles of political change."

There has been some difference of opinion, too, although not so vehement, on the literary, as differentiated from the philosophical, merits of the Declaration. Most of those who have criticized its literary worth are among those who condemned its philosophy, and based their criticisms on the vagueness with which certain generalities were expressed. Professor Tyler mentioned criticism of its "grandiose and vaporing style." But the vast majority of opinion on the literary merits of the document has been favorable and is well summarized by Dumas Malone, who wrote, in *Jefferson the Virginian:* "The literary excellence of the Declaration is best attested by the fact that it has stood the test of time. It became the most popular state paper of the American Republic not merely because it was the first, but also because to most people it has seemed the best. No other American document has been read so often or listened to by so many weary and perspiring audiences. Yet, despite interminable repetition, those well-worn phrases have never lost their potency and charm. So far as form is concerned, the continuing appeal of the Declaration lies in the fact that it is clear and simple and that, for all its careful craftsmanship and consummate grace, it was not so highly polished as to lose its edge. Only in its reiterated charges against the King does it even approach the declamatory. It may lack the stark grandeur of certain passages from Lincoln, it may be almost too felicitous; but it has notable elevation of spirit and solemnity of tone. Intended as an expression of the American mind, it was also Jefferson at his literary best."

The word most frequently used to describe Jefferson's writing is "felicity." The word is used in the sense of describing a knack for selecting the appropriate word or phrase or expression. He certainly handled the expression of the inalienable rights of man with much felicity in the phrase, "life, liberty, and the pursuit of happiness." Many other phrases in the Declaration can be picked out as examples of this quality in Jefferson's writing, among them: "a decent respect to the opinions of mankind"; "more disposed to suffer, while evils are sufferable, than to right themselves by abolishing the forms to which they are accustomed"; "for the sole purpose of fatiguing them into compliance with his measures"; "sent hither swarms of officers to harrass our people and eat out their substance"; "hold them as we hold the rest of mankind, enemies in war, in peace, friends."

Perhaps because of his writing style, Jefferson was a poor speaker. His reticence in public speaking made him, as a lawyer, dislike trying cases on the circuit. Although his ideas and his reason and logic were far superior, he could never face a jury with the confidence and conviction of his colleague, Patrick Henry. The reason, probably, was that his sensitive ear for the subtler, elusive harmonies of speech made him dissatisfied with what he had just said and think in terms of revising it, rather than of what he should say next. He instinctively wished to cross out the last sentence and say it over again with more felicity. In writing he could make changes and more changes until the sentences had the rhythm and cadence that made it the most appropriate expression of his thought. It might be said that he did not write; he composed. This is not to say that Jefferson was a labored writer. No man who wrote as much as he did could have done so with slow and painful effort.

His search for the right word, the right phrasing, is evident in the development of the first sentence of the second paragraph of the Declaration, from the rough draft to the document as submitted to Congress—and it must be remembered that the rough draft was probably not the first draft. In the rough draft the sentence looks like this:

> We hold these truths to be~self-evident~ sacred & undeniable; that all men are created equal & independent; that~ they are endowed by their from that equal creation they derive in rights~ creator with equal rights some of which are inherent & inalienable~ among which are the preservation of life, & liberty, & the pursuit of happiness.

In a sentence that finally contained thirty-six words, eighteen of the original words were eliminated and eleven substituted. The changes are obvious improvements. When Jefferson submitted the draft to Adams the only change was "self-evident" for "sacred and undeniable"; a change that may have been made by Franklin. Then he erased the words "and independent" probably to avoid two phrases ending with "ent" in close juxtaposition. The phrase "from that equal creation" became "they are endowed by their Creator," surely a more felicitous expression. But this phrase as he first wrote it was awkward in relation to what followed: "that they are endowed by their creator with equal rights some of which are inherent and inalienable among which are." There are too many whiches. So it becomes the much stronger and better-sounding phrase: "that they are endowed by their Creator with inherent and inalienable rights"—which finally became, simply, "unalienable rights."

The second paragraph in the Declaration, which Rufus Choate had particularly in mind when he referred to the document as "that passionate and eloquent manifesto" made up of "glittering and sounding generalities of natural rights" is, in fact, a clear and simple statement devoid of passion. The ideas in it could hardly have been expressed more concisely or in words more direct, simple, and appropriate, or, as Professor Becker says, "with less of passionate declamation, of rhetorical magniloquence, or of verbal ornament." This Jefferson critic makes the point that "apart from the peculiar felicities of phrasing, what strikes one particularly in reading the Declaration as a whole is the absence of declamation. Everything considered, the Declaration is brief, free of verbiage, a model of clear, concise, and simple statement. . . . The second paragraph of the Declaration of Independence reminds one of Lincoln's Gettysburg Address, in its unimpassioned simplicity of statement. It glitters as much, or as little, as that famous document."

Another good example of fecility in the Declaration is the last sentence as Jefferson wrote it, before Congress added "with a firm reliance upon the protection of Divine Providence." Perhaps the protection of Providence was important to the patriot cause, but the sentence as Jefferson originally wrote it—"And for the support of this Declaration we mutually pledge to each other our lives, our fortunes, and our sacred honor"—could hardly be improved. Professor Becker analyzes it thus: "It is true (assuming that men value life more than property, which is doubtful) that the statement violated the rhetorical rule of climax; but it was a sure sense that made Jefferson place "lives" first and "fortunes" second. How much weaker if he had written "our fortunes, our lives, and our sacred honor"! Or suppose him to have omitted "sacred"! Consider the effect of omitting any of the words, such as the last two "ours"—"our lives, fortunes, and sacred honor."

Elsewhere in the Declaration, Jefferson violated the laws of rhetoric. All books on the subject warn writers to avoid monotony and to seek a pleasing variety by alternating long and short sentences. Paragraphs, they say, should be devoted to a single idea, and more than one paragraph should never be made out of a single sentence. Jefferson violated all of these rules in his list of grievances against the King. He monotonously began each charge with the words "he has": "he has refused his assent," "he has forbidden his governors," "he has refused to pass laws," etc. And he deliberately started a new paragraph with each "he has". For Jefferson's particular purpose of drawing an indictment against the King, nothing could have served better than this repetitious list of evil deeds. Said Becker: "Nothing could be more effective than these brief, crisp sentences, each one the bare affirmation of a malevolent act. Keep your mind on the King, Jefferson seems to say; he is the man: 'he has refused'; 'he has forbidden'; 'he has combined'; 'he has incited'; 'he has plundered'; 'he has abdicated.' "

The opinion has been expressed that there is a doleful

quality about the paragraphs that surround the list of charges against the King, in such phrases as: "when in the course of human events"; "decent respect for the opinions of mankind"; "suffer while evils are sufferable"; "patient sufferance of these colonies"; "no solitary fact to contradict the uniform tenor of the rest." There is something in the cadence of these sentences that conveys a mournful sense of evils apprehended—long forfended and now unhappily realized. Said Becker: "Such phrases skillfully disposed have this result, that the opening passages of the Declaration give one the sense of fateful things impending, of hopes defeated, and injuries sustained with unavailable fortitude. The contrast in manner is accentuated by the fact that whereas the King is represented as exclusively aggressive, the colonists are represented as essentially submissive. In this drama the King alone acts—he conspires, incites, plunders; the colonists have the passive part, never lifting a hand to burn stamps or destroy tea; they suffer while evils are sufferable. It is a high literary merit of the Declaration that by subtle contrasts, Jefferson contrives to conjure up for us a vision of the virtuous and long-suffering colonists standing like martyrs to receive on their defenseless heads the ceaseless blows of the tyrant's hand."

After reviewing the emotional "philippic" against slavery, which Congress removed from the Declaration, Professor Becker summarizes his opinion of the literary qualities of the document thusly: "in the other parts of the Declaration, which have to do for the most part with an exposition of the constitutional rights of the colonies, or with a categorical statement of the King's violations of these rights, the appeal is more properly to the mind than to the heart; and it was in appealing to the reader's mind, of course, that Jefferson was at his best. Taking the Declaration as a whole, this is, indeed, its conspicuous quality; it states clearly, reasons lucidly, exposes felicitously; its high virtue is in this, that it makes a strong bid for the reader's assent. . . . The Declaration has not the grand manner—that passion under control which lifts prose to the level of true poetry. Yet it has, what is the next best thing, a quality which saves it from falling to the prosaic. It has elevation. . . . [Its] sentences may not be quite in the grand manner, but they have a high seriousness, a kind of lofty pathos which at least lift the Declaration to the level of a great occasion. These qualities Jefferson was able to communicate to his writing by virtue of possessing a nature exquisitely sensitive, and a mind finely tempered; they illustrate, in its subtler forms, what John Adams called his 'peculiar felicity of expression.' "

The qualities of simplicity, of clarity, of conciseness, of dignity are those that most literary critics have attributed to Jefferson's creation. Of the preamble, Dumas Malone wrote, "It is hard to see how Jefferson could have combined in such compass a larger number of important ideas or could have better imparted the tone of dignity, solemnity, respectful firmness, and injured virtue which the circumstances required. It was *necessary* to dissolve these old political bands. The American people were *entitled* to an independent station under the laws of God and Nature, but they had a *decent respect* to the opinions of mankind and were thus impelled to give reasons for their course.

And of the second paragraph: "before stating the specific reasons he took the whole controversy out of the realm of petty and selfish squabbling by setting it on a high background of philosophy. The philosophical passage in the Declaration, which he wrote as a single brief paragraph, became the most famous part of the document; and, as a summary of human rights and a justification of revolution in behalf of them, it is doubtful if it has ever been excelled."

Professor Moses Coit Tyler, in his *Literary History of the American Revolution*, makes the point that, unlike most writings that have the misfortune of being read too little, the Declaration has become hackneyed by generations of repetitions at Independence Day celebrations, which has "somehow confounded Jefferson's masterpiece with the rattle of firecrackers." Yet it has survived and attained its place in the minds of Americans only because of its supreme literary merits.

Said Professor Tyler: "Had the Declaration of Independence been, what many a revolutionary state paper is, a clumsy, verbose, and vaporing production, not even the robust literary taste and the all-forgiving patriotism of the American people could have endured the weariness, the nausea, of hearing its repetition, in ten thousand different places, at least once every year, for so long a period. Nothing which has not supreme literary merit has ever triumphantly endured such an ordeal, or ever been subjected to it. No man can adequately explain the persistent fascination which this state paper has had, and which it still has, for the American people, or for its undiminished power over them, without taking into account its extraordinary literary merits—its possession of the witchery of true substance wedded to perfect form—its massiveness and incisiveness of thought, its art in the marshaling of the topics with which it deals, its symmetry, its energy, the definiteness and limpidity of its statements, its exquisite diction—at once terse, musical, and electrical; and, as an essential part of this literary outfit, many of those spiritual notes which can attract and enthrall our hearts—veneration for God, veneration for man, veneration for principle, respect for public opinion, moral earnestness, moral courage, optimism, a stately and noble pathos; finally, self-sacrificing devotion to a cause so great as to be herein identified with the happiness, not of one people only, or of one race only, but of human nature itself. Upon the whole, this is the most commanding and the most pathetic utterance, in any age, in any language, of national grievances and of national purposes. . . . Indeed, the Declaration of Independence is a kind of war song; it is a stately and a passionate chant of human freedom; it is a prose lyric of civil and military heroism."

The Proclamation of the Declaration

For almost two centuries Independence Day has been celebrated on the wrong date. There is really nothing sacred about the fourth of July; nothing of great importance happened on that date, merely the adoption by Congress of the formal announcement of the resolution declaring independence that they had passed two days earlier. Presumably, we celebrate the fourth as the date on which the Declaration of Independence was *signed*, but it is very unlikely that anybody except Hancock and Thomson signed the document on that day.

On the third of July, 1776, John Adams wrote Abigail an uncanny prophesy of how Independence Day would be celebrated by future generations—but picked the wrong day. He wrote his wife: "Yesterday the greatest question was decided which ever was debated in America, and a greater, perhaps, never was nor will be decided among men. The second day of July, 1776, will be the most memorable epocha in the history of America. I am apt to believe that it will be celebrated by succeeding generations as the great anniversary festival. It ought to be commemorated as the day of deliverance by solemn acts of devotion to God Almighty. It ought to be solemnized with pomp and parade, with shows, games, sports, guns, bells, bonfires, and illumination, from one end of this continent to the other, from this time forward for evermore.

"You will think me transported with enthusiasm, but I am not. I am well aware of the toil and blood and treasure that it will cost us to maintain this Declaration and support and defend these States. Yet, through all the gloom, I can see the rays of ravishing light and glory. I can see that the end is more than worth all the means. And that posterity will triumph in that day's transaction, even although we should rue it, which I trust God we shall not."

When the copies printed by Dunlap were delivered to Congress, that body ordered that they be disseminated throughout the colonies with all dispatch, which, in those days, meant weeks before they reached the extremes of the country in Georgia and New Hampshire. Copies were to be sent to each of the assemblies of the newly independent states, to various committees and councils of safety, to commanding officers of militia, and, of course the Commander-in-Chief of the Continental Army in New York. The resolution said nothing about sending the Declaration to the newspapers; the people were to be reached mainly by copies that were to go out to "the ministers of each parish, of every denomination, to be read as soon as divine service is ended, on the first Lord's day after they shall have received." This was, in fact, a logical way of reaching the people. Not everybody read a newspaper, but everybody did go to church. After the clergymen read their copies, they were to be given to the clerk of the town council in each town, "who are hereby required to record the same."

The first newspaper publication of the Declaration was in the *Pennsylvania Evening Post* of July 6. The initial public proclamation was in Philadelphia, on July 8. John Hancock sent the Declaration to the Committee of Public Safety of Pennsylvania, on July 5, with a letter requesting them to "have [it] proclaimed in your colony in the way and manner which you shall judge best. . . . The important consequences flowing from the Declaration of Independence . . . will naturally suggest the propriety of proclaiming it in such a mode that the people may be universally informed of it." The Committee ordered the sheriff of Philadelphia to "read or cause to be read and proclaimed at the State House . . . the Declaration." At noon of that Monday, "The Committee of Safety, and Committee of Inspection, went in procession to the State House, where the Declaration . . . was read to a very large number of the Inhabitants of this city and county, which was received with general applause and heartfelt satisfaction."

That indefatigable correspondent, John Adams, left a record of the occasion, in a letter to Samuel Chase: "You will see by this Post, that the River is past and the Bridge cut away. The Declaration was yesterday published and proclaimed from that awful Stage, in the Statehouse yard, by whom do you think? By the Committee of Safety!, the Committee of Inspection, and a great Crowd of People. Three Cheers rended the Welkin. The Battalions paraded on the common, and gave Us the Feu de Joy [*sic*], notwithstanding the Scarcity of Powder. The Bells rung all Day, and almost all night. Even the Chimers, chimed away. The Election for the City was carried on amidst all this Lurry with the Utmost Decency, and order . . . in the evening our late King's coat of arms was brought from the Hall, in the Statehouse, where the said King's Courts were formerly held, and burned amidst the acclamations of a crowd of spectators."

The location that Adams defined as "that awfull stage" was the platform or balcony of an observatory, "twelve to fifteen feet square, at fifty to sixty feet south of the [State] House," which the scientist David Rittenhouse is supposed to have had erected to observe a transit of Venus. As with so much else relating to events of national portent during the first days of July, 1776, there is some difference of opinion as to certain details of this proclamation. Christopher Marshall wrote in his diary: "Warm sunshine morning. At eleven, went and met Committee of Inspection at Philosophical Hall; went from there in a body to the lodge; joined the Committee of Safety (as called); went in a body to State House Yard, where, in the presence of a great concourse of people, the Declaration of Independence was read by John Nixon. The company declared their approbation by three repeated huzzas. The King's Arms were taken down in the Court Room, State House same time. From there, some of us went to B. Armitage's tavern; stayed till one. I went and dined at Paul Fook's, lay down there after

dinner till five. Then he and the French Engineer went with
me on the commons, where the same was proclaimed at each
of the five Battalions. . . . Fine starlight, pleasant evening.
There were bonfires, ringing bells, with other great demonstrations of joy upon the unanimity and agreement of the
declaration."

Other eyewitnesses disagree about the size of the crowd
and the identity of the reader. One says: "The Declaration
was read by Captain John Hoskins." History prefers Nixon
to Hoskins because he was a member of the Committee of
Safety and because a copy of the printed Declaration, which
now hangs in Independence Hall, was found among Nixon's
effects by his granddaughter, and is possibly the copy from
which he read. It has been theorized that Captain Hoskins
may have read the Declaration to the five battalions of
militia later in the day.

As to the crowd, Charles Biddle wrote in his autobiography; "On the memorable Fourth of July, 1776, I was in the
old Statehouse yard when the Declaration of Independence
was read. There were very few respectable people present.
General **** spoke against it, and many of the citizens who
were good Whigs were much opposed to it; however, they
were soon reconciled to it." Biddle obviously confused the
fourth with the eighth of July. The name of the general
who spoke against it is obliterated, but the reference is believed to be to General Dickinson speaking against the Declaration in Congress, not in the Statehouse yard. A girl who
later became Mrs. Deborah Logan and who also heard the
reading confirmed Biddle's comment on the lack of respectable people in the crowd. She wrote: "The first audience of
the Declaration was neither very numerous or composed of

the most respectable class of people." This reference to respectability undoubtedly had to do with people of wealth and social position rather than people of good virtue. Most of the former class in Philadelphia were Tories who obviously would have stayed away from the assemblage. Jefferson was probably one of the not respectable who was there, although he never mentioned the occasion.

The Declaration was proclaimed in several nearby towns on the same day, including Easton and Trenton. On July 9, it was read at Princeton, where, it was said: "Nassawhall was grandly illuminated, and INDEPENDENCY proclaimed under a triple volley of musketry, and universal acclamation for the prosperity of the UNITED STATES. The ceremony was conducted with the greatest decorum." On the same day it was read in New Brunswick. The account of this proclamation left by Charles Deshler is probably typical of what happened in hundreds of towns throughout the new nation:

"When the Declaration of Independence was brought to New Brunswick, I was a boy about nine years old. There was great excitement in the town over the news, most of the people rejoicing that we were free and independent, but a few looking very sour over it. . . . The Declaration was brought by an express rider, who was at once furnished with a fresh horse, and despatched on his way to New York. The County Committee and the Town Committee were immediately convened, and it was decided that the Declaration should be read in the public street (Albany Street), in front of the White Hall tavern, that the reader should be Colonel John Neilson, and that the members of the two committees should exert themselves to secure the attendance

of as many as possible of the staunch friends of independence, so as to overawe any disaffected Tories, and resent
any interruption of the meeting that they might attempt.
Although these Tories were not numerous, they were, most
of them, men of wealth and influence, and were very active.
Accordingly, at the time appointed (I cannot now recall
the hour, if, indeed, my grandfather stated it), the Whigs
assembled in great force, wearing an air of great determination. A stage was improvised in front of the White Hall
tavern, and from it Colonel Neilson, surrounded by the
other members of the committee, read the Declaration with
grave deliberation and emphasis. At the close of the reading
there was prolonged cheering. A few Tories were present;
but although they sneered, and looked their dissatisfaction
in other ways, they were prudent enough not to make any
demonstration."

Late the same day, July 9, General Washington received
copies of the Declaration in New York and issued an order:
"The several brigades are to be drawn up this evening on
their respective Parades, at six oclock, when the Declaration
of Congress, shewing the grounds & reasons of this measure,
is to be read with an audible voice. The General hopes this
important Event will serve as a free incentive to every officer, and soldier, to act with Fidelity and Courage, as know-
ing that now the peace and safety of his Country depends
(under God) solely on the success of our arms."

The troops are said to have been drawn up in hollow
squares in Lower Manhattan, within sight of the English
forces on Staten Island and the British fleet in the bay. One
participant recalled that Washington sat his white horse in
the center of one of the squares as the Declaration was read.

The general left only this brief and uninspired account of the incident in a letter to Congress: "Agreeable to the request of Congress, I caused the Declaration to be proclaimed before all the Army under my immediate Command, and have the pleasure to inform them, that the measure seemed to have their hearty assent; the Expressions and behaviour both of Officers and men testifying their warmest approbation of it."

After the reading, it would seem that the taverns did a good business. In any event, that evening, a crowd led by some Sons of Liberty decided to tear down the largest statue in the New World, the equestrian figure of George III, in Bowling Green. John Adams in his *Diary* recalled: "Between the fort and the city is a beautiful ellipsis [*sic*] of land railed in with solid iron, in the centre of which is a statue of his majesty on horseback, very large, of solid lead gilded with gold, standing on a pedestal of marble, very high." Contemporary sketches show the crowd hauling at this, with ropes around the neck and pushing it with poles. The purpose was undoubtedly patriotic, but Washington did not like his troops engaged in vandalism. Next day his orders contained the admonition: "Tho the General doubts not the persons, who pulled down and mutilated the Statue, in the Broadway, last night, were actuated by Zeal in the public cause; yet it has so much the appearance of riot and want of order, in the Army, that he disapproves the manner and directs that in future these things shall be avoided by the Soldiery, and left to be executed by proper authority."

Most of the statue was hauled in wagons to Litchfield, Connecticut—there is no explanation of why it was taken so

far away. Here, under the supervision of signer Oliver Wolcott, the ladies of the town melted it down for musket balls.
An accounting of this shows that most of the work was
done by "Mrs. Marvin, Ruth Marvin, Mrs. Beach, Laura,
Mary Ann and sundry persons"; although the latter sundry
persons made only 2,182 of the 42,088 "cartridges" that the
statue produced. One correspondent recorded: "The King
of England's statue has been pulled down to make musket
balls so that his troops will probably have melted Majesty
fired at them."

Legend has it that the head of the statue was mounted on
a pole outside a tavern near Fort Washington, until two
intrepid loyalists stole and buried it. After the British captured New York, it was unearthed and sent by Colonel
James Montrésor to England. He recorded: "I rewarded
the men and sent the head by the *Lady Gage* to Lord
Townshend, to convince them at home of the infamous disposition of these people."

At Boston the proclamation of the Declaration took place
two weeks after it had been adopted. Abigail Adams left
one account of it: "I went with the multitude to King
Street to hear the proclamation for independence read. . . .
The troops appeared under arms, and all the inhabitants
assembled there—the smallpox prevented many thousands
[coming in] from the country—when Colonel Crafts read
from the balcony the proclamation.

"Great attention was given to every word. As soon as he
ended, the cry from the balcony was: God save our American states! Then three cheers rent the air; the bells rang; the
privateers fired; the forts, the batteries, and cannon were

discharged; the platoons followed. And every face appeared joyful. . . .

"After dinner, the King's arms were taken down from the State House and burned in King Street. Thus ends royal authority in this state. And all the people shall say Amen."

A somewhat more detailed record was left by a British officer on parole in Boston: "As we passed through the town, we found it thronged. All were in their holiday suits. . . . The streets were lined with detachments of infantry, tolerably equipped. In front of the Court Street Jail, artillery was drawn up, the gunners standing with lighted matches . . . the town clerk read the Declaration from the balcony to the crowd outside. At the close, a shout, begun in the hall, passed to the streets, which rang with loud huzzas, the slow measured boom of cannon, the sharp rattle of musketry. . . . There was a banquet in the Council Chamber, where all the richer citizens appeared. Large quantities of liquor were distributed among the mob. When night closed in, the darkness was dispelled by general illumination.

"In front of the tavern on the upper corner of State and Kilby Streets, all portable signs of royalty—such as the arms from the State House, Court House, Customs House, whether lion and crown; pestle, mortar, and crown; or heart and crown—were taken down and thrown in a pile to make a bonfire."

And so it went throughout the nation until the Declaration finally reached Savannah, Georgia, aboard a ship on August 10. Here, according to a newspaper account, the Declaration was first read by the "honorable council" in their chamber: "They then proceeded to the square before the assembly house, and read it to a great concourse of people, when the grenadier and light infantry companies fired a general volley. After this, they proceeded to the liberty pole. . . . At the liberty pole they were met by the Georgia battalion, who, after the reading of the Declaration, discharged their fieldpieces, and fired in platoons. Upon this they proceeded to the battery, at the trustee's gardens, where the Declaration was read for the last time, and the cannon of the battery discharged.

"His Excellency and council, Colonel Lachlan McIntosh, and other gentlemen, with the militia, dined under the cedar trees, and cheerfully drank to the UNITED, FREE, AND INDEPENDENT States of America. In the evening the town was illuminated, and there was exhibited a very solemn funeral procession, attended by the grenadier and light infantry companies, and other militia, with their drums muffled, and fifes, and a greater number of people than ever appeared on any occasion before, in that province, when George the Third was interred before the courthouse."

Subsequent celebration of July Fourth as Independence Day, and the nature of such celebrations probably developed from these initial proclamations. The document that was read to the crowds was headed: "In Congress, July 4th, 1776," and this date, rather than the actual date on which the resolution of independence was passed, remained in the public mind as the occasion for a celebration. The discharges of musketry and cannon of the original celebration became firecrackers in later years, and the "illuminations" that marked the initial events became the town fireworks displays of today. Until recently, patriotic speeches by politicians, during which the Declaration was read—or at least its beginning and end—were an important, albeit frequently dull, part of the festivities. The annual celebration of Independence Day seems to have started in Philadelphia, in 1778. There is no record that the first anniversary was publicly noted.

The document itself—that is, the engrossed, signed, parchment copy—traveled a weary road, until it was finally enshrined as a sacred relic in 1924. During approximately the first half century of its existence, it was not treated as though it had any particular significance. It presumably remained in the hands of Charles Thomson and followed Congress in the wanderings of that body during the war. Toward the end of 1776, as the British neared Philadelphia, Congress fled to Baltimore and here the Declaration was printed for the second time. This was the first edition to contain the names of the signers. Congress fled again in 1777, first to Lancaster and then to York, Pennsylvania, where the Declaration was stored, with other state papers, in a courthouse. It came back to Philadelphia with Congress in the spring of 1778, and remained in the Statehouse until 1783, when it again followed Congress to its successive seats in Princeton, Trenton, Annapolis, and New York, where it was stored in City Hall.

When Washington was inaugurated as the first President, in 1789, the Secretary of Congress turned the Declaration over to him to be placed in the custody of the Secretary of State when there was such an individual. John Jay had it for a while as acting secretary and then it came back into the hands of its creator when Thomas Jefferson returned from France to become the first Secretary of State. Jefferson probably stored it in his office on Lower Broadway until the government moved to Philadelphia for ten years, starting in 1790. Upon Jefferson's retirement as Secretary of State, in 1794, it passed into the hands of successive secretaries, who may or may not have unrolled it. The document arrived in the sea of mud that was the new Federal City, Washington, D.C., in the custody of John Marshall, in 1800. The State Department had inadequate storage facilities and for the next fourteen years the Declaration lay in the War Office Building.

In 1814 the Declaration took a hectic trip when the British invaded Washington. There are many dramatic legends about it, but the rather prosaic truth is that the Secretary of State, James Monroe, had the papers of his department packed in linen sacks and removed to safety well before the British arrived. The Declaration stayed one night in a barn and was then transferred, with the rest of the State Department papers, to the home of a clergyman, named Littlejohn, in Leesburg, Virginia, where it remained until the British departed and the government returned to the capitol. It got its first permanent home in 1820, in the new State Department Building, on the site of the present Treasury.

Meanwhile, following the War of 1812, which confirmed American independence, the document started to take on something of its sacred character. In 1816 two individuals undertook, as commercial ventures, to publish facsimile editions of the Declaration, with signatures. The first was issued by a penman named Benjamin Owen Tyler, who copied the signatures so well that Richard Rush, the son of the signer, who was then Secretary of State, could not distinguish them from the originals. The second engraved edition came off the press of John Binns, a few months later. This had not only signatures but the seals of the thirteen states and, at the top, pictures of Jefferson, Hancock, and Washington. It is not clear why Washington's likeness was included, since he had nothing to do with the Declaration, but no one seemed to object. In 1823, Secretary of State John Quincy Adams had the first official facsimile engraved, of which two copies were sent to each of the surviving signers, Jefferson's being on parchment. Copies were also sent to important personages throughout the nation.

By this time the Declaration was beginning to deteriorate physically; no effort had been made to preserve it. Fortunately, it had never been folded, but rolling and unrolling it on numerous occasions had had an adverse effect, particularly to the signatures that were at the bottom—and thus received more wear and tear. Its condition was not improved when, in 1841, it was for some reason placed in the new Patent Office Building, where, for a generation, it hung on a wall, in a frame exposed to light from an opposite window. Fading and yellowing were inevitable under these conditions and, by the time the document was taken to Philadelphia for exhibition at the Centennial Exposition, in 1876, many of the signatures were so dim that they were hardly recognizable and some had completely faded from view. At the time, there was much talk of restoring the document, either by manually retracing the writing, or with chemicals, but nothing came of this.

After the Exposition, the Declaration was displayed in the State Department, rather casually, until 1894, when the necessity for protecting it from further exposure to uncontrolled conditions was finally recognized. It was sealed between two plates of glass and placed in a safe in the State Department, where it remained in obscurity for a quarter century. In 1921 it was transferred to the Library of Congress, quietly, in a mail truck. Here, it lay in the office of the Librarian of Congress for three years, while a shrine was being designed and built for its public display, together with the United States Constitution, hermetically sealed tween sheets of glass and exposed only to diffused, indirect light. It was officially put on display on February 19, 1924, with a little ceremony attended by President Coolidge.

It was believed that the Declaration had reached a final resting place, but the attack on Pearl Harbor upset this reckoning. As a safety measure, the two precious documents were transported to Fort Knox, and stored with the nation's gold in an underground vault. There they remained until the fall of 1944, during which time the Declaration was inspected and reconditioned by experts from the Department of Standards. In October, 1944, both documents were brought back to their shrine in the Library of Congress.

In 1952 a new building was constructed for the National Archives as a depository for the official records of the government. Obviously, these records included the Declaration of Independence and the Constitution, so a special hall was included in the building to house and display these relics. So, on December 13, 1952, the Declaration made what is hoped is its last trip; this time in a tank escorted by guards from all branches of the armed services, from the Library of Congress to the National Archives. Here, it is now on display, together with the Constitution, sealed in a vacuum of insulated glass.

Perhaps the most memorable celebration of the Declaration of Independence was its fiftieth anniversary, because it was on this day—July 4, 1826—that the man who had written it and the man who had fought for it on the floor of Congress died within a few hours of each other; Jefferson at eighty-three and John Adams at ninety-one. Political differences had estranged them for some ten years after Jefferson replaced Adams in the White House, but, in their final years, largely through the efforts of co-signer Benjamin Rush, they had become reconciled and carried on a correspondence that involved some of the most precious letters of each of these Founding Fathers. In one, Jefferson wrote on the meaning of the great event in which both had played leading roles:

"I shall not die without a hope that light and liberty are on steady advance. We are destined to be a barrier against the returns of ignorance and barbarism. Old Europe will have to lean on our shoulders and hobble along by our side. . . . We have seen, indeed, once within the records of history, a complete eclipse of the human mind, continuing for centuries. And this, too, by swarms of the same northern barbarians, conquering and taking possession of the countries of the civilized world. . . . But even if the clouds of barbarism and despotism should again obscure the science and liberties of Europe, this country remains to preserve and restore light and liberty to them. The flames kindled on July 4, 1776, have spread over too much of the globe to be extinguished by the feeble engines of despotism. On the contrary, they will consume these engines and all who work them."

And again, upon hearing of the death of Dr. Rush, Jefferson wrote: "Another of our friends of '76 is gone, another of the co-signers of the independence of our country. And a better man than Rush could not have left us, more benevolent, more learned, of finer genius, or more honest. We, too, must go, and that ere long. I am the only one left, south of the Potomac. . . . I have sometimes asked myself whether my country is better for my having lived at all. I do not know that it is. I have been the instrument of doing certain things. But they would have been done by others, some of them perhaps a little better."

As the Fourth of July neared in Quincy, Massachusetts, a committee called at the farmhouse of John Adams to request that the ex-President give a toast, to be used at the local celebration of the anniversary. Standing on his porch, the old man said, "I will give you a toast. I give you: Independence forever."

"Have you nothing to add to that, sir?" he was asked.

"Not one word," replied the old man.

Three days later, John Adams quietly died. A few moments before his death, he murmured, "Jefferson still survives." But Jefferson did not still survive. A few hours before, he had expired at Monticello, first having written an epitaph for his tombstone, which listed his three greatest contributions to humanity, as he conceived them, headed by his authorship of the Declaration of Independence:

> Could the dead feel any interest in Monuments or other remembrances of them . . . the following would be to my Manes [i.e. soul or spirit] the most gratifying.
> On the grave
>   a plain die of cube of 3 f. without any mouldings,

surmounted by an Obelisk of 6 f. height, each of a
single stone:
On the faces of the Obelisk the following inscription, & not a word more

"Here was buried
Thomas Jefferson
Author of the Declaration of American Independence
of the Statute of Virginia for religious freedom
& Father of the University of Virginia."

because by these, as testimonials that I have lived,
I wish most to be remembered.

Someone had conceived of a great celebration for the
fiftieth anniversary of the Declaration of Independence, to
be attended by the three surviving signers: Thomas Jefferson, John Adams, and Charles Carroll of Carrolltown. Jefferson's last reference to the Declaration was written ten
days before his death, to decline this invitation. In it he
wrote:

"I should, indeed, with peculiar delight, have met and exchanged there congratulations personally with the small
band, the remnant of that host of worthies, who joined with
us on that day in the bold and doubtful election we were to
make for our country, between submission or the sword;
and to have enjoyed with them the consolatory fact, that
our fellow citizens, after half a century of experience and
prosperity, continue to approve the choice we made. May
it be to the world, what I believe it will be (to some parts
sooner, to others later, but finally to all) the signal of arous-
ing men to burst the chains under which monkish ignorance
and superstition had persuaded them to bind themselves, and
to assume the blessings and security of self-government.
That form which we have substituted restores the free

right to the unbounded exercise of reason and freedom of
opinion. All eyes are opened, or opening, to the rights of
man. The general spread of the light of science has already
laid open to every view the palpable truth; that the mass of
mankind has not been born with saddles on their backs, nor
a favored few booted and spurred, ready to ride them legiti-
mately, by the grace of God. These are grounds of hope for
others. For ourselves, let the annual return of the day forever refresh our recollections of these rights, and an undiminished devotion to them."

Index